REFLECTIONS ON THE BEATITUDES

By the same author

Did You Receive the Spirit?
Prayer
The Way of the Preacher

REFLECTIONS ON THE BEATITUDES

Soundings in Christian Traditions

by

SIMON TUGWELL, O.P.

Darton, Longman and Todd
London

First published in Great Britain in 1980
Darton, Longman & Todd Ltd.
89 Lillie Road
London SW6 1UD

© 1980 Simon Tugwell, O.P.

ISBN 0 232 51467 4

Nihil obstat: Fergus Kerr, O.P.
Timothy Radcliffe, O.P.

Imprimi potest: Jonathan Fleetwood, O.P. (Provincial)
22 November 1979

Printed in Great Britain by The Anchor Press Ltd.
and bound by Wm Brendon & Son Ltd.
both of Tiptree, Essex

Man was made for Joy and Woe
And when this we rightly know
Thro the World we safely go
Joy & Woe are woven fine
A Clothing for the Soul divine
Under every grief & pine
Runs a joy with silken twine

William Blake
Auguries of Innocence, 56–62

Contents

Introduction

This book grew out of a retreat. It is not intended to be a work of scientific exegesis, and I can make no claim to any expertise in that field. I hope that there are no exegetical howlers, but my primary concern has been to use the beatitudes as a starting point for reflection on what it means for us to be followers of Jesus Christ. This reflection has been nourished by all kinds of dippings into the traditions of the church, so I appeal in a variety of ways to a variety of writers from many periods of Christian history, and, since the church does not exist in isolation from the rest of the human race, I have also sometimes appealed to sources which are not Christian, and these, too, come from a variety of ages and localities. I make no claim to have discovered anything particularly new, nor would I dream of suggesting that what I have found is anything like exhaustive. St Ephrem the Syrian bids us drink what we need from the living water of scripture, but never to imagine that we have drained that water dry. There is plenty left for us when we return later, and plenty left for others to discover.[1]

There are many people who have helped me on my way in the making of this book. I must mention in particular the Daughters of the Cross in Hayle, Cornwall, to whom I preached the retreat which is the origin of the book. They very kindly taped all my talks, thereby providing me with a basis of text on which I could work. I am grateful to my publisher for getting these tapes transcribed. I have since then used the opportunity of several other retreats to return to this basic text, and I must thank the sisters of various communities for putting up with the sound of the typewriter during their retreats, and for the help they gave me, often quite unconsciously, by their interest and reactions; the communities in question are: the Dominican sisters in Burnt Oak and in Portstewart, and the Sisters of Mercy in Rochfortbridge. In addition to these, many other groups of religious, clergy and laity have served as sounding boards for my ideas on the beatitudes over a period of several years, and, though I cannot now list them all, I am deeply indebted to them.

I must also express my gratitude to several of my own brethren who have generously given their time to read through my typescript in various stages of its development, in particular Gareth Moore, O. P., Timothy Radcliffe, O. P., Fergus Kerr, O. P. and Brian Davies, O. P. Benedict Green, C. R. was kind enough to cast an expert exegetical eye over the whole text, and I am indebted to his scholarly comments for deliverance from several blunders and oversights; if what I say is still sometimes eccentric, the fault is mine, not his. I am also grateful to Dr Sebastian Brock for checking my translation from St Ephrem's Syriac.

For those who are interested, I have tried to indicate in my notes where my sources, whether quoted or simply mentioned, can be found and explored, with reference to critical editions, where such exist, and to modern translations, except where they are so easy to find that it would be superfluous to give more details. I have also occasionally used the notes to quote from or to refer to additional material which seemed to me to be interesting, but not sufficiently important or directly relevant enough to merit admission to the actual text of the book. It is my hope that nobody need be frightened by the apparent burden of learning in these notes; they are not essential for a reading of the book. They are intended, in the first place, for those who, like myself, find it annoying to be left in the dark about where alleged texts come from; but I also hope that there may be some readers whose appetites will sometimes be whetted by what they find in my book so that they wish to make further sorties into the riches of Christian tradition. I have tried to give such people sufficient guidance to facilitate their further study. Finally, should anyone with scholarly interests happen to read this book, I hope that the notes will be adequate to convince him that my appeals to traditional sources and to occasional modern writers are not made frivolously or tendentiously.

Unless it is specified otherwise, all translations in this book, including those of scripture, are my own.

Oxford   SIMON TUGWELL, O. P.
22 November 1979

A INTRODUCTORY

Chapter One

There is no doubt that the beatitudes have played a quite special role in Christian thinking about life. Bossuet places them at the beginning of the meditations which he put together for the use of his Visitation nuns, saying, 'If the sermon on the mount is the précis of all Christian doctrine, the eight beatitudes are the précis of the whole of the sermon on the mount.'[1] St Dominic is said to have prayed especially for the gifts of the Holy Spirit to be given to the Order he had founded 'so that both he and his brethren might find it their joy and delight to live in the spirit of the beatitudes.'[2] The connexion between the beatitudes and the gifts of the Holy Spirit was made first by St Augustine, who also worked in the seven petitions of the Lord's Prayer.[3] Medieval theologians who preferred a more stratified view of life declared that the beatitudes outline a perfection even higher than that promised by the gifts of the Spirit.[4] The compilers of the present lectionary of the Roman Church could find no text more appropriate than this for the Feast of All Saints.

Nevertheless, the beatitudes make a puzzling text. And the more one thinks about them, the more puzzling they become. On the one hand, they obviously call us to a tremendous height of spiritual and ethical achievement, to a righteousness which goes even further than that of the scribes and Pharisees (such as the Lord requires of his disciples—Matt. 5:20); yet, at the same time, they seem almost to canonize qualities which are the very antithesis of all achievement and success.

This is, of course, a paradox which we find elsewhere in the New Testament. Christian maturity is not just a matter of pulling ourselves together and being very impressive characters who have got it all right, who know exactly what it means to be a Christian and

1

who have the will-power and the staying power actually to live up to it.

St Paul might seem to be a decidedly strong-willed person; yet he wrestled and wrestled in vain with his mysterious 'thorn in the flesh'. When he pleaded to be rid of it, the Lord only answered him, 'My grace is enough.' St Paul had to learn that it is precisely in weakness that strength is made perfect (2 Cor. 12:7–9). Our strength is the strength of God, but the strength of God given to man and so revealed curiously in weakness.

And it was surely from the experience of this that St Paul learned to talk even about the weakness of God (1 Cor. 1:25). God does not come into our world with the toughness of an omnipotent thug, to sort everything and everybody out. He himself has chosen the way of weakness. There is something about God which is better expressed in weakness than in strength, in foolishness than in wisdom, in poverty than in richness. The story of the earthly life of Jesus Christ is a story of human failure, of human poverty, of human foolishness. And yet that is the revelation of God in human terms. And we who are followers of Jesus Christ are called to be imitators of him, and so should not be at all surprised to find that one of the arts we have to learn is the sublime art of weakness.

That certainly does not mean that we should simply be complacent in our weakness and think that there is no room for effort. There is plenty of evidence in the writings of the saints and in the bible that there is a very real place for effort. But effort can be misplaced.

St Paul, on the basis of his own experience as a Pharisee and as a Christian, gives us an important statement of the nature of Christian perfection. He claims that, as a Pharisee, he had achieved the kind of righteousness enshrined in the Jewish law, as understood by the Pharisees: he was, he says, 'blameless according to the righteousness which is in the law' (Phil. 3:6). But, as a Christian, he has no further use for that kind of righteousness, for that kind of accomplishment.

It is all too easy for us to treat the Pharisees as embodying all that is worst in humankind. But in fact they were probably the best men of their time, the most religious, the most devoted to the will of God, the most eager to express their loyalty to him in obedience to his every word, the most determined never to compromise with

2

the world around them. But, as St Paul came to see it in retrospect, they were exposed to a fatal flaw: the trouble with their outstanding righteousness was that, all too easily, it could be viewed precisely as *their* righteousness. It was a righteousness that could be measured, so that, at a certain point, you could say that you had now achieved it. This meant that it could all too easily come adrift from its original inspiration in devotion to God and become self-sufficient, an end in itself.

But how tempting it is to define righteousness in such a way that we can, at least conceivably, one day declare ourselves to have arrived at it. How lovely it would be to be able to go striding boldly into church, like the Pharisee in the Lord's parable, and say, 'I thank you, God, I am doing splendidly' (cf. Luke 18.10ff). How humble we should be, how ready to acknowledge that it was all due to God's grace—and yet how insufferably conceited, and how abysmally dull.

The requirements of the Lutheran polemic have, to some extent, obscured the real objection that is being brought against the Pharisees. It is not they they are laying claim to some righteousness that they have achieved *on their own*, in opposition to a righteousness conceded by the grace of God. There is no suggestion in the Lord's parable that the Pharisee is being hypocritical in thanking God for his own happy condition. So far as we can tell, the Pharisees were probably quite prepared to acknowledge their dependence on God's grace; there are some early Rabbinic texts which express such dependence in the most emphatic terms.[5] Of course there is the risk that human beings will forget their dependence on God, and this is a part of St Paul's complaint; but the far more essential criticism is that the Pharisaic concept of righteousness is such that it allows a man to be self-consciously righteous, to contemplate himself in his righteousness, to treat it as something he can possess as his own, whether or not he also thinks that he has achieved it on his own.

The basic form of complacency, after all, is that a person is pleased with himself. Someone may quite easily be complacent about his or her gifts, even while acknowledging that they are gifts. We can be self-satisfied about our good looks or our intelligence without having to suppose that we have created them ourselves. It is only a subdivision of complacency to be smug because we take full credit for ourselves to ourselves.

3

And complacency can enter even into our humility. Even when we go to confession, we can, more or less surreptitiously, be concerned with our own image of ourselves.

In Graham Greene's novel, *The Power and the Glory*, the whiskey priest on one occasion interrupts an old woman penitent who is prattling on and tells her:

> 'Remember your real sins.' 'But I'm a good woman, father,' she squeaked at him with astonishment. 'Then what are you doing here, keeping away the bad people?' He said, 'Have you any love for anyone but yourself?' 'I love God, father,' she said haughtily. He took a quick look at her in the light of the candle burning on the floor—the hard old raisin eyes under the black shawl—another of the pious—like himself. 'How do you know? Loving God isn't any different from loving a man— or a child. It's wanting to be with Him, to be near Him.' He made a hopeless gesture with his hands. 'It's wanting to protect Him from yourself.'[6]

If all else fails, we can even get a certain smug joy out of watching our own honesty, our own self-exposure, our own humiliation.

The point was raised formally in a medieval controversy about the essential content of heavenly bliss. Durandus of St Pourçain, a Dominican noted for his opposition to orthodox Thomism, maintained that what the blessed enjoy immediately and directly is not God, but their own vision of God. He suggests a comparison with a man's love of wine: it is not the wine, as such, that satisfies him, but his drinking of the wine.[7]

This view is very firmly refused by Meister Eckhart, who is followed and, indeed, quoted on the matter by Bl. Henry Suso.[8] The reflex movement of self-consciousness would be a distraction from the beatitude of simply knowing God. According to the text in St John (17:3), eternal life is in knowing God, not in knowing that we know God. It is not that we are unconscious of our own knowledge of God or of our bliss; but the consciousness of ourselves is not the actual object of our bliss, it is not that that actually makes us happy.

Discussion of what heaven is like is, perhaps, never going to obtain for us all that much clarity about eternal life, because we cannot really conceive of it so long as we are still bound by the conditions of life in this world. Maybe in that *tota simul possessio*[9] in

4

which all the particular kinds of enjoyment which we now know only in separation from one another form only one complete enjoyment, some kind of self-consciousness which might be noxious as a distinct phenomenon in itself will be fully innocent and appropriate. But the usefulness of attempting to make projections about eternity is that they can help us to focus on the trends which are discernible in different kinds of approach to life on earth. Can we really envisage spending eternity gazing at our own contentment, saying to ourselves, 'There! I made it!'? In its own way, that is just as absurd as Agatha Christie's character who cannot imagine heaven as being anything other than a continual occasion for her to make herself useful. The only picture of herself that she can really enjoy is the picture of herself as the devoted servant of her loved ones (who, of course, have either to evade or to endure with as much good grace as they can the unceasing persecution of her devoted service).[10]

The danger with our good works, our spiritual accomplishments, and all the rest of it, is that we shall construct out of them a picture of ourselves in which, effectively, we shall situate our happiness. Complacency in ourselves will then replace delight in God.

St Paul's concept of Christian perfection is radically incompatible with this kind of complacency, because it forces our attention constantly away from ourselves and our achievements and obliges us to look ahead, to God in whom all goodness dwells. His goal is

> to gain Christ and to be found in him, not having any righteousness of my own from the law, but having the righteousness which exists through faith in Christ, the righteousness which comes from God and is built on faith.

He makes no claim, as yet, to have arrived at his goal; what he does is simply to forget what lies behind and stretch out to what lies ahead. And it is precisely this, he says, that is the proper attitude for those who 'are perfect'. Perfection means the continual striving ahead, not any conviction of achievement (Phil. 3:12–15).

This model of perfection is developed at length by St Gregory of Nyssa, especially in his *Life of Moses*. The only definition of virtue, he says, is that it is undefined, unbounded.[11] Moses' ascent into the darkness on Mount Sinai is taken as a symbol of the ascent of the soul of man, constantly going beyond itself and beyond all kinds of

5

imaginative or conceptual representation of God.[12] And this process never ends. At no point can we say, 'That's it.' St Gregory even envisages eternity like this.[13] Maybe this is not an acceptable view of eternity, but it is a valuable projection because of the light it sheds on temporal life.

It is with a similar concern, surely, to disqualify complacency that our Lord tells us, when we have done everything we ought to have done, not to pat ourselves on the back, but to say, 'We are useless servants' (Luke 17:10).

And this is at least part of the point of the saying that we must become like little children, if we want to enter the kingdom of God (Matt. 18:3). In all three synoptic gospels there is what is surely meant to be a significant contrast implicit in the juxtaposition of the scene with the little children and the story of the rich man who wants to know what he should do to inherit eternal life. The rich man seemingly has everything; not only has he got wealth, he is evidently a thoroughly good man, who has kept all the commandments since he was young. (It is only in Matthew that he is said to be still a young man.) The Lord loves him as soon as he sees him. But he sends him away with a flea in his ear, for all that, commenting, 'How hard it is for those with money to enter the kingdom of God.' The disciples are dumbfounded. 'Then who can be saved?' they ask. This rich man would seem to be the ideal candidate for eternal life. But maybe that is the whole point. The message that our Lord wishes to put across is precisely that, however well placed we are, it is still, quite strictly, *impossible* for us to enter the kingdom of God. When the disciples ask who can be saved, the only answer they get is, 'It is impossible with men, but not with God' (Mark 10:13ff etc.).

The rich man wanted to discover something he could *do* in order to inherit eternal life, he wanted to keep himself in the picture. But there is nothing that any of us can do. We must simply *receive* the kingdom of God like little children.[14] And little children are precisely those who have not done anything. The ancient world was not sentimental about children and had few illusions about any pretended innate goodness in them. The Lord is not suggesting that heaven is a great playground for Arcadian infants. The children are our model because they have no claim on heaven. If they are close to God, it is because they are incompetent, not because they are

6

innocent. They contrast with the rich man simply because there is no question of their having yet been able to merit anything. If they receive anything, it can only be as a gift.

When our Lord tells us to become like little children, he is bidding us forget what lies behind. Children have no past. Whatever we have done in the past, be it good or evil, great or small, it is, strictly speaking, irrelevant to our stance before God. It is only *now* that we are in the presence of God. And 'now', as de Caussade brings out, is always a 'desert',[15] in which we can have no sense of where we have got to. It is from our past and from our attempts to programme the future that we insert the present into some kind of picture of our lives and ourselves. But in the naked 'now' there is no room for any picture of ourselves. And that is where God is. We may, if we like, prefer to call it 'nowhere'.[16]

'Look, I am making everything new,' declares the risen Lord in the great vision of the Apocalypse (Apoc. 21:5). We cannot bring the luggage of our past with us into the new moment of God's making.

The past is, perhaps, not totally lost, but it is no longer ours; it is in the hands of God and is his business. It will be retrieved in the *tota simul possessio* of eternity, but should not be stored away on earth. As far as we are concerned, we must realize that we are like children, at the beginning, not the end, of a road. Whatever past achievements might bring us honour, whatever past disgraces might make us blush, all of these have been crucified with Christ; they exist no more except in the deep recesses of God's eternity, where good is enhanced into glory and evil miraculously established as part of the greater good.

As we grow older, we inevitably acquire an ever-increasing past. The danger is that we shall see ourselves and present ourselves too much in terms of that past. This is why we are generally so much concerned to have some kind of interpretation of our own past ready at least for our own use. Most of us probably spend quite a lot of time 'editing' our autobiographies, so that we shall have the 'official version' of the story ready for judgement day.

But does it really matter? Are we not just wasting our time? Do we have to justify or excuse or commend ourselves like this? Can we do it anyway? Is it all really not just designed to safeguard our complacent contemplation of our own picture of ourselves?

'Look, I am making everything new.' The newness of God calls for and calls forth a corresponding newness in us. Our anxious totting up of our past shows a misconception of what it means for us to be confronted with God. This is why the stories of death-bed conversions are so important a part of Christian tradition; we are not, in the final analysis, our past, we are whatever we are in God's present.

We must not misinterpret this as signifying that we ought, in principle, to be able to verify empirically that we are new like children at every moment of our lives. It is a theological statement that we are making, not a psychological one. There is no reason to suppose that we shall *feel* new. There clearly can sometimes be miraculous interventions which do create an entirely new situation, so that a state of affairs which had seemed insoluble suddenly rights itself or turns into something else; but we should certainly not presume on such miracles happening. And that is not only because it is never safe to presume on miracles happening, but also because if we did set up this particular kind of miracle as normative, we should be in serious danger of falsifying an important point of doctrine. If we were led to believe that somehow we ought to *feel* new the whole time in our relationship with God, we should simply be re-establishing a new pattern of the kind of Pharisaism rejected by St Paul; we should be defining the criteria for a successful response to God, and so would end up with exactly the same hazard of complacency, even if the particular criteria of success were slightly different (laws of psychological wholeness or spirituality rather than laws of Mishnah).

One of the consequences for most of us of growing older (and I am not referring to becoming old—the process begins before we can walk or talk) is that we develop a sense of how one thing leads to another, and that makes it possible for us to become calculating, 'If I do this, then I shall be in a good position for getting or achieving that.' What we have to realize, and it is a difficult point for us to grasp, is that there is no such thing as a 'good position' in our dealings with God.

Meister Eckhart in particular keeps on reminding us that we must grasp God in *everything*.[17] Anyone who insists on approaching God in any particular way 'gets the way, but lets go of God'.[18] We must be completely detached about all circumstances, external and internal; we must even be detached about detachment.[19] The truly spiritual person does not even seek tranquillity (of whose importance Eckhart elsewhere speaks in emphatic terms[20]), because he is in no way hampered by lack of it.[21] So all possible answers we might give to the question, 'What shall I do to inherit eternal life?' are declared irrelevant and counter-productive; we are given no encouragement at all to entertain our feeling that if only we did not get these headaches, if only we had nicer neighbours, if only we knew how to pray, if only we were more humble, everything would go swimmingly.

We do not have to work out how to get ourselves into a good position for having a relationship with God, we do not have to design ways of explaining our position to him, we do not have to create a pretty face for ourselves, we do not have to achieve any state of feeling or understanding. The newness inherent in any situation of encounter with God is brought by him, not by us, and the newness it calls for in us is not a newness of physical or psychological or intellectual experience, it is simply a newness of being given to him (and that, too, is not a matter of psychological or any other kind of experience in itself, though it may, of course, lead to or involve some kind of transformation of our experience of life).

So, to return to the paradox with which we started, the beatitudes do indeed draw for us a picture of a kind of spiritual perfection and ethical achievement, but it is a kind of perfection which will be, almost by definition, not self-conscious of itself as perfection or achievement. It is a kind of perfection which even seems to render useless the whole familiar distinction between success and failure, achievement and non-achievement, which is such an important instrument in our normal analysis of life.

But then, what should we expect? If God is to be the measure of our perfection, and we are bidden to be 'perfect as your heavenly Father is perfect' (Matt. 5.48), how could we ever begin to evaluate our progress, let alone commend ourselves on our development?

The stretching of righteousness beyond that of the Pharisees must profoundly alter our very concept of what it means to be righteous and even more of what it feels like to be righteous. If it is open-ended towards God, towards divine perfection, then it is no longer possible to reduce it to what can be quantified. Of course, a quantifiable element remains: it is still right and proper for us to say

9

that murder is a sin, and that therefore abstaining from murder is a good thing. But such things no longer add up to a definition of righteousness, not even a working definition. When we have done all that we ought to have done and refrained from all that we ought to have refrained from, we are still only useless servants. And if we have done all that we ought not to have done and failed to do all that we ought to have done, our position is equally or almost equally unclear. Though it took many centuries for the church to arrive at our present position in which it is shockingly easy for, say, a murderer to be in good standing in the church, this has surely been a healthy development. The easiness of confession for every class of sinner, whatever problems it may cause to the relatively squeamish tastes of most believers, is an important attestation of the nature of our relationship with God in Christ.

As abba Theodotus said, 'Do not judge a fornicator if you are chaste, otherwise you will be transgressing the law too. For he who said, "Do not fornicate," also said, "Do not judge." '[22]

We are all, equally, privileged but unentitled beggars before the door of God's mercy.

Chapter Two

The beatitudes draw for us a very strange picture of the man who is blessed: he is poor and unimpressive, hungry and in mourning, trodden on, yet able to make peace. Most of these are qualities that it is very difficult for us to live with, or at least to live with realistically, as applied to ourselves. Either we shall instinctively think of 'those poor', when we think of the poor at all, and then, as likely as not, move on to a rather condescending concern to improve their lot; or we shall indulge in a highly dramatic version of 'I in my poverty and pain' and go ranting round the stage like a badly produced Ibsen hero.

It is hard for us to say, 'Yes, I am poor,' and to say it simply, and it is even harder to say it and then leave it at that, without the rider, 'And something has got to be done about it.' (And that 'something' need not always mean relief of our poverty; the Ibsenesque hero wants applause, not relief.)

Either way, our reaction is conditioned by a sense of outrage, of indignation. We do not like what we see, and therefore have to try to turn it into something else, or at least to exploit it to bring about something we can approve of more easily.

But 'God saw all that he had made and behold, it was good, very good' (Gen. 1:31). That fundamental approbation at the dawn of creation was never withdrawn. The neat, schematic presentation of things in the first creation story underpins the whole of biblical revelation. The tension at times becomes almost unbearable; God wants even to obliterate all that he has made (Gen. 6:7). But the appeal back to his original covenant can never fail. For all his wrath, his fundamental favour stands for ever.

The Lord's eyes are 'too pure to see evil' (Hab. 1:13). He does not know the way of the wicked (cf. Ps. 1:6). But that does not

11

mean that God is blind, that he is incapable of noticing most of what goes on in his world. It means that he cannot see evil simply as evil. He cannot see anything simply with indignation. The approbation of the sixth day, the day on which man was made, is taken up agonizingly into the sacrificial love of that other sixth day, the day of *Ecce homo* (man made, man accepted, man revealed), the day of Calvary. Those eyes which looked on all that they had made and saw it as good, looked out from the vantage point of the cross and saw that same world, and saw it with that same relentless love. The sabbath of God must be observed, even if it has to be observed in a tomb. The Lord rested from his labours.

And from that rest, the world begins anew.

God, too, knows how to be outraged; but his outrage is not like ours. Ours comes from seeing evil. His comes from seeing good, and seeing it, impossibly, co-existent with that which is less good. God, too, knows how to yearn to change things, to make all things new; but the newness he makes does not contradict the goodness he already sees. For him the 'last things', the new things, are 'like the first things', the old things.[1]

The adage of the ancient metaphysicians, *ens et bonum convertuntur*, becomes in theology a defiant declaration of faith. Whatever is, *is* good, notwithstanding any evidence to the contrary.

Charles Williams, in his analysis of the fall and of redemption, points out that when man learns from the devil to know good and evil, this involves his coming to see good as evil; there is nothing but good for him to see or know. If he is to know evil, it can only be by a distorted vision of what is good. That is how evil is conceived and, in due time, brought to birth.

God's retort is to see evil as good. Charles Williams traces the development of the response to evil: at first, the most that is offered is a certain forgetting of evil. Sin shall be reckoned as if it had not happened. But that can at best be only a makeshift, temporary solution to the problem. Even God cannot make never to have happened that which has in fact happened.[2] The definitive answer, prepared in the silence of eternity and revealed in the passion of Christ, is that evil itself must become a part of good.[3]

It is some vague sense of this, surely, that lies behind the philosophical and mystical speculation, and more recently, psycho-ana-

12

lytical speculation, about a condition which is beyond good and evil, in which the venerable dualism is overcome and transcended.

It is not enough simply to resist evil, to try to blot it out. Evil does not have sufficient ontological consistency of its own to be thus radically disentangled from things, so that you could separate it off and destroy it. Evil is a quality of things that are good, and a merely negative response to it entails, practically, a negative response also to the things that are good.

A basic element in our conversion is, paradoxically, that we must change our attitude to that which we must recognize as less than good, in ourselves and in our circumstances.

Jewish tradition, aware that there is in our make-up an impulse towards evil as well as an impulse towards good, nevertheless insisted that both impulses must be counted among those things which God saw in his creation as being 'very good'.[4] Man must accordingly learn to love God with all his heart and soul and mind, including his evil impulse.[5]

It is a mistaken view of our position in God's world to suppose that we could have an unalloyed purity of motivation in this life. The Letter of Barnabas regards it as one of the more dangerous temptations for the Christian to regard himself as being already justified, already made righteous.[6] In the view of this author, the fundamental objection to the Jewish observance of the sabbath is that God commanded us to observe the sabbath with clean hands, and we have not yet got clean hands. This must mean that we have not yet reached the point at which the sabbath can be celebrated.[7]

In fact, we have not yet reached the sabbath at all, in one sense. God has not yet finished his creation. 'My Father is working until now, and so am I' (John 5:17). Pseudo-Barnabas, in line with this conviction, asks us whether we can honestly apply to ourselves all that is said in the bible about Adam. Can we rule the fish and the other animals, as Adam is supposed to be able to do? If not, that means that we have not yet entered into our full human inheritance. We are still in the process of being made. Before we become 'Adam', man in God's image and likeness, we must increase and grow.[8]

The vital thing for us, now, is that we should not anticipate what is still to come. We must not presume on a perfection and completeness that is yet to be achieved. We must acknowledge that we

13

are still a mixture of old and new. We must not be lulled by a false complacency into 'going to sleep over our sins'.[9]

There can be little doubt that pseudo-Barnabas is largely concerned to alert his readers to the danger of some sort of Judaising, and his comments go well with the New Testament picture of the Pharisees. As we have seen, the real objection to the Pharisee in our Lord's parable of the Pharisee and the publican is not that he feels superior (though that is significant), but that he is using a concept of righteousness which allows him to feel himself to be righteous. It is on that basis that he can also feel himself to be superior. The competitive element is secondary and is dependent on the self-consciousness.

And, of course, it is difficult, almost intolerable, for us to live with the awareness of ourselves as other than wholly good, successful, happy, strong and so on.

That is why we find it so hard to live with ourselves in truth. We should prefer to live with someone we could admire more wholeheartedly. So we try to present ourselves in some way that we can admire. And so we deceive ourselves.

And so, at the outset of any true conversion, we have to 'return to ourselves'. In the parable of the prodigal son we are told that, in his misery, he 'returned to himself' (Luke 15:17 Vulg), and it is here that St Augustine finds a key to man's whole return to God.[10] Man seeks everywhere for God and does not find him, because he seeks everywhere except where he himself is. But that is where God is. When man returns to himself, he finds God there, waiting to be gracious to him (Isa. 30:18).

In St Vincent Ferrer's *Treatise on the Spiritual Life* the one thing which is stressed as the foundation for all the rest is just this return to ourselves. Its name is humility. We must know what we are. We must see 'more clearly than daylight' that we have no source of good or of accomplishment in ourselves. We must abandon the whole attempt to be something impressive or even mildly prepossessing in our approach to God. We must learn to live with the deepest possible conviction of our own worse than nothingness. Only so can God make anything genuinely beautiful out of us.[11]

About two months before she died, St Thérèse of Lisieux exclaimed, 'How happy I am to find myself imperfect and so much in need of the good God's mercy at the time of my death!'[12]

This is not quite the same thing as suggesting that we should be complacent about our weaknesses. To be complacent about ourselves is, however perversely, to feel ourselves to be acceptable.

The task ahead of us is to know ourselves as not acceptable. And to accept that knowledge.

We must learn the art of weakness, of non-achievement, of being able to cope with the knowledge of our own poverty and helplessness, without trying to escape from it into something we can accept more easily. And we must know that it is even in that poverty and helplessness that God sees us, and sees us with love, even with approbation, however much it may be tinged with regret and censure. God never says to us, 'I want you to become something else' without also saying, 'I love you as you are!'

In our meditations on the beatitudes it is quite crucial that we keep on bringing them back to ourselves, reminding ourselves that 'this means me.' It is not 'they' who are poor, it is I myself. And what is being said is not, 'those poor, poor people, what can we do about it?' but 'you blessed poor people, blessed are you.'

Whatever else they may be, then, the beatitudes are a call to us to see ourselves, to live with ourselves, in a way that probably does not come easily to most of us, and to forgo an enterprise that is generally dear to us, the enterprise of getting ourselves into a position where we can see ourselves in a 'good' light. Christian righteousness or rightness with God does not *feel* like righteousness, and we should not devote our energy to bringing ourselves into a position that feels right. It is when we feel ourselves to be poor, humiliated, desperate and all the rest of it that we qualify for the label 'blessed'.

B   ANTIDOTE VIRTUES

Chapter Three

Blessed are the poor in spirit,
for theirs is the kingdom of heaven.

St Matthew and St Luke present this beatitude in slightly different forms. St. Luke's is the cruder and perhaps the more basic: 'Blessed are you who are poor.' It is twinned with a corresponding woe: 'Woe to you who are rich' (Luke 6:20, 24).

There is a kind of material crudeness about this which should not be overlooked. It is the same message that we find elaborated in the parable of Lazarus and the rich man (Luke 16:19ff): if you prosper in this world, you will pay for it in the next; and vice versa. We may moralize it if we please, but we are given few grounds for doing so in the text itself. Maybe the rich man in the parable could have been nicer to the poor man at his gate, but that is not what Abraham objects against him. The point of the story as it is told is not that Lazarus was a good man and the rich man bad, but simply that the one was rich and the other poor, and that in the next world their roles are reversed. And that is all. Woe to you who are rich.

The lack of subtlety in this is rather startling, but it is not without parallels in Jewish literature. Rabbi Judah the Prince is said to have taught quite simply that 'He who accepts the pleasures of this world shall be denied the pleasures of the world to come; but he who does not accept the pleasures of this world shall be granted the pleasures of the world to come.'[1] It was apparently a common proverb among the Jews that not everyone is privileged to 'eat at both tables'.[2]

There is an abundance of anecdotes to illustrate the principle, such as the story of Rabbi Hanina who was very poor and who was one day badgered by his wife to pray for some relief. At once a hand appeared and presented him with a golden table leg. 'Thereupon he saw in a dream that the pious would one day eat at a three-legged golden table but he would eat at a two-legged table.'[3]

All of this is, of course, in marked contrast to the belief of at least the earlier portions of the Old Testament. There piety and prosperity go together. Material rewards are the expected consequences of keeping God's law (e.g. Deut. 6:3; 11:13ff).

The problem is posed acutely in the book of Job as to whether this earlier view is adequate to cope with the reality of life in this world. Job is presented as being a man as good as can be. Yet he is struck down by one catastrophe after another. His 'friends' insist that he must have sinned, otherwise his situation would be unintelligible. Job is equally insistent, and it is essential to the author's purpose that we believe him in this, that he has not sinned. But this leaves us with a situation we are surely meant to see as intolerable and nonsensical, in which an innocent man suffers every kind of loss and hardship. At the end of the story Job is in fact restored to worldly prosperity, but in the meantime he has to have his concept of God shattered to be replaced by a far more profound and vast idea of God.

It is really only in the intertestamental period that Judaism begins to develop a sense that material prosperity does not necessarily go with piety, and that, maybe, it is even typical that the man who is devoted to the law of God should be among the poor and downtrodden of the world.

At first, no doubt, this was simply a factual observation. But in time it became a positive doctrine that the righteous man must not expect to prosper in this world, and this is probably to be connected with the growing sense that this present age is the age of the dominion of Satan. Jewish piety at this period, probably under the influence of Iranian doctrines which the Jews had met during their exile, began to operate with a sharp dichotomy between this present age and the age to come. It is the latter which is God's age, when his servants will be rewarded.[4]

Early Christian thought took over this concept. There is a widely attested belief that this world, as we know it now, is subject to the 'Ruler of this world' (cf. John 14:30).[5] There goes with it a sense of the real danger that prosperity in this world can be had only on the terms of the Ruler of this world.

This is the position indicated in the frightening vision which the

17

Apocalypse gives us of what is to come before the end of our world. A time is there envisaged in which only those who bear the mark of the Beast will be able to be engaged in commerce and trade (13:17). The whole economic system is controlled by the enemy of God. One of the consequences, therefore, of fidelity to God must be a radical dissociation from the whole financial order of the world.

In the Apocalypse this state of affairs is presented as being still in the future. But the same warning is applied even to the present in the Shepherd of Hermas:

> You servants of God should know that you are living in a land which is not your own. Your own city is a long way from this one. So, if you know your own city in which you are going to dwell, why are you acquiring fields here like this and expensive establishments and buildings and unnecessary homes? Anyone who makes this kind of provision for himself in this city is evidently not expecting to return to his own city. You idiotic ditherer, do you not realise that all these things belong to someone else and are subject to his control? One day the lord of this city will say to you: 'I refuse to have you living in my city; leave this city, because you do not follow my laws.' With your possession of fields and houses and all your many other properties, what will you do with your land and your home and all the rest of your wealth when you are thrown out like this? The lord of this land is quite right in what he says: 'Either follow my laws or leave my country.' So what are you going to do? You have your own law in your own city. Will you completely deny your own law, because of your fields and other possessions, and live by the law of this city?[6]

In Hermas' view this is one of the greatest risks facing the Christian. Of all sins, that of denying God's covenant and throwing off one's allegiance to it is the most disastrous. And it is precisely this that is likely to result from worldly possessions, because they are always liable to provoke a conflict of loyalties.[7]

A similar image is used in the Gospel of Thomas:

> Mary said to Jesus: 'Whom are thy disciples like?' He said: 'They are like little children who have installed themselves in a field which is not theirs. When the owners of the field come, they will say: "Release to us our field." They take off their clothes before them to release the field to them and to give back their field to them.'[8]

18

The mythical trimmings in these texts should not lead us to ignore the seriousness of the doctrine. It is a very real question for all of us, how far we can expect to achieve worldly success of any kind at all without compromising our fidelity to God. There is a very fine and difficult distinction between using the mammon of unrighteousness to win friends for ourselves who can usher us into eternal life (Luke 16:9) and attempting to serve God and mammon (Matt. 6:24).

There is no room here for puritanism or fastidiousness. As Barnabas reminded us, it is not possible for us in this world to have completely 'clean hands'. The 'talent' we have to trade with is always going to be, to some extent, tainted; there is no currency other than 'mammon of unrighteousness'. If it really comes to a showdown, then, as the church has always known, the outcome is either apostasy or martyrdom. But in the meantime we must accept that there is a question mark hanging over all our undertakings in this world. In whatever way we are inserted into society, we are going to run the risk of serving mammon. This is just as true of seemingly 'good works', such as education, as it is of obviously worldly enterprises like making money. Whatever we are trying to do in this world, to some extent we shall unavoidably find ourselves influenced by the prescriptions of the world.

The church has obviously never been able to draw systematically radical or rigorous conclusions from this and insist on total alienation from society for all her members. There has always been room for wealthy and successful believers.[9] But they need to heed the warning that their very salvation depends on their generosity to the genuinely poor. As Hermas says, it is the prayers of the poor that win salvation for the rich.[10] *Mutatis mutandis*, something similar must surely be said about all of us who are in any way viable members of worldly society; our salvation depends on our being in effective fraternity with society's rejects, however such fraternity is expressed.

All the same, however important it is not to spiritualize this principle out of existence, it is equally important not just to turn it into a merely this-worldly concern to identify ourselves with any particular social, political or economic group. The division into 'rich' and 'poor' from the point of view of God's kingdom cannot be that simply translated into mundane categories. All of us are to some extent worldly successes, and all of us are to some extent worldly rejects, if only because the world has no universally agreed criteria of acceptance or rejection.

The essential thing is that we do not lose sight of the warning that we are unlikely to be allowed to eat at both tables. This is a principle of very wide application, as we can see, for instance, from the way in which our Lord uses it in connexion with people who make a great parade of their piety in order to impress the world around them. Our Lord's comment is simply, 'They have their reward' (Matt. 6:2, 5).

Now, from this point of view, it does not make very much difference what kind of short-term objective we have. We may be out to commit murder or to reform the British economy; once we have achieved our objective, we 'have our reward'. There may be some reason to hope that people will devote themselves to reforming the economy rather than to murder, but strictly from the point of view of beatitude, they are both insufficient objectives, and therefore capable of deflecting us from our way to God's kingdom. The question mark is still there: should it come to the crunch, which matters more to us: God or our success in reforming the economy?

The complete or relative incompatibility between prosperity and success (of whatever kind) in this world and prosperity in the world to come is certainly the immediate context for our beatitude. But it does not exhaust for us, any more than it did for St Matthew, the significance of the beatitude of the poor.

Elsewhere in the sermon on the mount our Lord makes another very down-to-earth observation about earthly property, 'Do not store up for yourselves treasure on earth,' he says (Matt. 6:19), and in addition to the moral factor involved he reminds us that in any case we *cannot* very successfully store up treasure for ourselves on earth. It simply does not work. Even if we manage to preserve our goods from the inroad of moths and rust and burglars, we cannot preserve them very long for ourselves, simply because we cannot preserve ourselves to enjoy them. In another story that he told, our Lord ridiculed a man who built himself enormous barns to hoard his crops in: that very night he was visited by death. 'Fool, tonight they want your soul off you. And this property of yours, whose will it be now?' (Luke 12:16ff).

20

In this world we cannot, in any serious way, possess anything, because things are not secure enough and we are not secure enough. We live in time, we live in a world, therefore, that systematically flows away. As Heraclitus is popularly supposed to have said (but probably did not), 'You cannot step into the same river twice.'[11] By the time you have stepped into it for the second time, it is not the same river and you are not the same person. And this is paradigmatic of everything. To quote another famous remark which Heraclitus probably did not make, 'Everything flows.'[12]

And so the attempt to catch things and hang on to them, to say, 'Right, that's mine, I've got it!' is fundamentally misconceived. 'The fashion of this world passes away' (1 Cor. 7:31); when St Paul bids us 'use this world as if we did not use it', he is simply being realistic.

When we are young and healthy, and when the sun is shining, there is perhaps nothing terribly difficult about this philosophy. 'Gather ye rosebuds while ye may,' as Herrick bids good-looking young ladies.[13] But when the rosebuds have gone, what then? And what when 'time's winged chariot'[14] has caught up with us and we are weak and weary and cannot gather the rosebuds?

If the gospel has no more to say to us than that we should make hay while the sun shines, it is consigning us to bitterness of soul when the sun stops shining. And if it is only telling us to wait patiently for the sun to shine in heaven, offering us pie in the sky in return for misery here below, it is at best a dingy kind of message.

Maybe it was to clarify this that the beatitude was expanded to read, 'Blessed are the poor in spirit.' What is at stake is not just our relationship to material possessions, it is a whole question of our attitude, our spirit. The redirection of our attention from earthly to heavenly coffers must not be taken to leave unchallenged our very concept of what possession means.

It is instructive in this connexion to look carefully at the story of the fall of man. The serpent tempts Eve with the promise that if she will eat fruit from the tree of knowledge 'your eyes will be opened and you will be as God, knowing good and evil' (Gen. 3:5). The subtlety of this is brought out, presumably deliberately, by the later creation story added by the so-called Priestly writer, in which it is stated that God made man, male and female, 'in his own image and likeness' (Gen. 1:27). That is to say, it is not simply a temp-

21

tation to man to wish to be like God; he is meant to be like God. But he is meant to be like God by virtue of God's creating him that way, not by virtue of some human act of appropriation. What the serpent is offering is not something in itself wrong, then, it is rather a distortion in the mode of possessing something which is already there and which is good. It is a new concept of ownership that he is seeking to instil.

Likeness to God was something that God had given to man, but originally there was nothing that man had done to appropriate it and make it his own. Indeed, what was there that he could have done? How could he secure his ownership of something that must always be God's gift? Why, in any case, should man wish to make sure like that? Why should he wish to make his own possession of likeness to God an object of his attention in its own right?

It is Satan who suggests that they should *do* something to become like God, that they should take their likeness to God into their own hands. The gesture of taking the fruit and eating it is an obvious symbol of a man taking something into his own hand and then storing it away safely inside himself. It is a symbol of that security of possession which has become such an obsessive concern of fallen man.

Further security can then be sought, security, perhaps, of a slightly different kind, by insisting on the contrast between possession and non-possession. We want to be able to draw the line between having and not having. The Pharisee in the Lord's parable bolsters up his own sense of what he has by contrasting himself with others who do not have what he has.

Things like this build up our concept of possession. And what a pernicious concept it turns out to be! How often do we experience its futility, in fact, and yet how hard it is to learn the lesson. How many friendships and marriages have been destroyed by it, by possessiveness and exclusiveness. One sure way to lose friendship, whether in family relationships or anywhere else, is to try to hang on to it too tightly. It can be possessed only in so far as it is constantly received as a gift which is ever new. There is something radically insecure about real having, something that should not be regarded as 'a pity', it is one of the real beauties of God's ordering of things. But fallen man has lost the taste for that kind of insecurity.

He likes things he can hang on to—or thinks he can, because in fact, of course, as we have seen, this is a vain hope.

It is really only the poor in spirit who can, actually, have anything, because they are the ones who know how to receive gifts. For them everything is a gift.

The Lord told another parable about this, or partly about this. It is a story about a man who goes away, leaving a certain amount of money with his servants. One of the servants very prudently wraps the money up and buries it. He wants to be sure he does not lose it (Matt. 25:14ff). He is typical of fallen man. He wants to take no risks. But precisely because of this, he loses the talent which had been entrusted to him. The master wanted his servants to take risks. He wanted them to gamble with his money.

The Lord calls us to the poverty of being always ready to relinquish everything that is given to us, so that it can be given back to us enhanced and multiplied. Unless we are prepared to play the game of time like this, and risk losing everything, even what we thought we had will be taken away from us sooner or later. To try to 'possess' in that way is in fact to possess nothing.

'Blessed are the poor in spirit, for theirs is the kingdom of heaven.' The reason why it is so important for us to unlearn the kind of possessing that the devil taught us is that, ultimately, the only thing worth possessing is utterly beyond all possessing. Traherne, in his *Centuries*, ridicules the mean-mindedness which confines us to some few possessions that we can regard as our own and nobody else's. *Everything* is meant to be ours, as indeed St Paul had said (1 Cor. 3:22). And in this totality of 'possession', our rights can only be enhanced by those of everyone else; it is a completely different concept of possession. But anything less than this is just silly, in face of the abundance that might be ours.

Would one think it Possible for a man to Delight in Gauderies like a Butterflie, and Neglect the Heavens? Did we not daily see it, it would be Incredible. They rejoyce in a Piece of Gold more than in the Sun: and get a few little Glittering Stones and call them Jewels. And Admire them because they be Resplendent like the stars, and Transparent like the Air, and Pellucid like the sea. But the stars them selvs which are ten thousand Times more usefull Great and Glorious, they Disregard.[15]

Were all your Riches here in som little place: all other Places would be

Empty. It is necessary therfore for your Contentment, and true Satis-faction, that your Riches be Dispersed evry where. Whether is more Delightfull; to have som few privat Riches in one, and all other Places void, or to hav all places evry where filled with our Proper Treasures?. . . To hav a few Riches in som narrow Bounds, tho we should suppose a Kingdom full, would be to hav our Delights Limited, and Infinit Spaces Dark and Empty, wherin we might wander without Satisfaction. So that God must of necessity to satisfy His Lov give us infinit Treasures. And we of Necessity seek for our Riches in all Places.[16]

Meister Eckhart, in a very different style, makes much the same point, when he says that God cannot give us little bits: he can only give everything at once or nothing at all.[17]

As long as we are playing the diabolical game of 'possessing', we can never get beyond this and that, beyond the little bits that God cannot give. We could never encompass the kingdom of heaven, so as to 'possess' it. It is only when we have gone through the discipline of re-appraising everything in terms of the precariousness of gift, that we can become capable of the true and total gift of God.

And what does it mean for the kingdom of heaven to be ours? It is evidently not something which we could ever exhaust by any definition, but it must surely indicate a state of affairs in which our lives are centred on God, structured by his mode of being himself and his mode of acting.

And here we reach the ultimate depth of the beatitude of poverty of spirit.

For God is himself only in pouring himself out. We cannot fathom the whole mystery of God, plainly, but whatever we can know is characterized by this total giving of self. The Father bestows the fullness of Godhead on his Son. There is, according to the traditional Christian doctrine, nothing of what it means to be God that the Father reserves to himself. And the Son does not consider equality with God, with the Father, something to be grabbed, something to be tightly held on to (Phil. 2:6). He, too, pours himself out. What we know most immediately is his outpouring of himself for our sake in the incarnation; but this is surely correctly seen as the manifes-tation in time and in human nature of his eternal, divine being for the Father. His final sacrifice of himself for us on the cross is

24

expressed as a yielding of himself into the hands of his Father (Luke 23:46).

We can, if we like, talk of the Father and the Son possessing their common Godhead; but it would be at least as true to talk of their dispossessing themselves of it in each other's favour. They are God in giving themselves to each other. And that gift is the source of the proceeding of the Gift, the Holy Spirit.

If it is a law of all created being that everything flows, that nothing can strictly be held fixed in possession, that is because it is a law of uncreated being that everything flows. The divine life itself comes to be defined as a life of *perichoresis*, and however dead the metaphor becomes in the jargon of the theologians, the image of circular *movement* is always latent within it.[18] God possesses himself only in the continual exchange between the three Persons.

Thus it is not just as a remedy for sin that we are taught that if we, who are made in the image of God, would preserve our lives, our souls, we must lose them (Matt. 10:39). It is built into our very nature that we can only possess ourselves, like God, in giving ourselves.

According to one tradition of exegesis, it is strictly 'male and female' that is in the image of God. A man without his wife is not in the image of God.[19] And there is surely an element of truth in this. Not necessarily that only a union of man and woman constitutes the image of God in us; but some kind of giving of ourselves to others is involved in it. It is in the unity of believers in Christ that the unity of God is reflected (John 17:11). Man, as St Basil said, is not 'a monastic animal'.[20] It is not good for him to be on his own (Gen. 2:18).

But, because of sin, this law of self-giving has become a law of death. Because man set about trying to possess what could not be possessed, he has painfully to learn how to be dispossessed. It no longer comes pleasantly to him to lose his own life in order to live.

And we should not be too coy about adopting the other possible translation of the Greek phrase: we must be prepared to lose our own *souls*. If we are too much concerned even with our own eternal salvation, there is a risk that that very concern will defeat its own end. If we are too much concerned to accumulate spiritual treasures for ourselves, we shall make ourselves incapable of receiving the gift of God's kingdom.

How much more will this be true if we are too much concerned with our own emotional, intellectual condition? We must be prepared to be dispossessed of all that we understand by life, if we would truly live.

The reason for this is, of course, not that it would be *greedy* or selfish to demand emotional and intellectual and physical well-being. The true reason is almost precisely the opposite, in fact. It is to do with the sadly neglected virtue of magnanimity, greatness of heart.[21] There is something rather poky and cramping about insisting on our well-being. Not much observation is needed, really, to discover this to be so. One of the surest ways to avoid being happy is to insist on being happy at all costs. The religion of cheerfulness, as Father Brown reminds us, is 'a cruel religion'.[22] And maybe the best way not to go mad is not to mind too much if you do go mad. There is an element of hazard involved in nearly everything worth while. If you want to explore life on the other side of the road, you have to surrender the security you have on the pavement and brave the risk of getting run over. And the hazard increases proportionately to the worth-whileness.

In response to the rather meagre demands that we often make, our Lord declares, 'It has pleased your Father to give you the kingdom' (Luke 12:32). Our expectations must expand, to become at least more adequate to God's purpose for us. It is no good our saying, 'All I wanted was a little piece of toast.'[23] There is a devilish humility which besets us at times which is probably far more damaging than a great deal of pride. It has pleased our Father to give us a kingdom. Our lesser aspirations, even our aspirations towards emotional, intellectual, physical, even spiritual well-being may sometimes have to be sacrificed, not because they are too demanding, but because they are not demanding enough. Christianity is not just a sophisticated programme of psychological self-improvement. It is eternal life that is at stake. And it is for this that our timidly clutching fingers must be prised open. All disordered self-possession must be unlearned, if we are to be made truly blessed. We must be weaned from ourselves and our grip on ourselves. And the normal way in which we are weaned is by being exposed to situations of mental, emotional and spiritual deprivation. Western Christian spirituality has come to speak of this process in terms of 'dark nights' of the senses and of the spirit, and these have sometimes been contrasted with what is alleged to be the rather less gloomy spirituality of the Christian East. But eastern spirituality, however different its terminology, is every bit as concerned to eliminate the disorders that have wrecked the stability and integrity of our lives, and if some eastern Christian spiritual writers seem less brutal in what they say, it is only because they are less pessimistic about human cooperation in the weaning process than some of their western counterparts. The more man resists, the more he will be hurt, and western Christians have, perhaps, become more resistant and so have thrown up a more savage kind of spirituality. But the aim of the exercise is the same throughout.

And finally, we must even be weaned from 'God'. Meister Eckhart says, 'I pray God to rid me of God.'[24] And in this he situates the ultimate poverty. And we might find here also the ultimate imitation of God. 'My God, my God, why have you abandoned me?' (Matt. 27:46). We must lose God if we would find God. Of all sins, perhaps the most insidious and the hardest to eliminate is that of idolatry. What St Paul said of the Athenians can be said, in one way or another, of fallen mankind as a whole: 'I see that you are very religious' (Acts 17:22). All of man's instincts have become warped, but not annihilated, by sin, and that includes his instinct for God. Man cannot banish God from his life, however hard he tries. He needs a god. But, so long as he is wedded to the programme of possessiveness laid down by the serpent at the beginning of all our woe, he will accept only a god whom he can possess as an object.

But God is not an object.

God make me rid of 'God'! Any 'God' that I can treat as an object, any God that I can make my own, is a false god. God is only 'God' over against creatures; he is named, to distinguish him from other beings,[25] but precisely as such he is not apprehended as he really is. That is why the soul cannot, finally, be content with 'God'. As Meister Eckhart puts it:

> The highest and most intimate renunciation that a man can practise is that he should renounce God for God's sake. Now Saint Paul renounced God for God's sake; he renounced everything that he could have received from God and everything that God might have given him. In renouncing

27

all this, he renounced God for God's sake, and what remained to him was God as God essentially is in himself, not in the manner of being received or won, but in that essence which God is in himself. He gave God nothing nor did he receive anything at all from God. It is a Unity and a pure Uniting.[26]

The infinity of God's reality can no more be caught by my possessing than I could catch a hurricane in a shrimping net.

Blessed are the poor in spirit, those who have allowed themselves to be stripped of the old spirit, the spirit of acquisitiveness and 'security', for theirs is the kingdom of heaven, because they no longer seek to possess, but to be possessed, to lose themselves and all that is 'theirs' in the ecstasy of simple receiving and simple giving again, or, more accurately, without even any giving or receiving, in the simple being which is the authentic image in us that divine ecstasy of being which is the living God.

Chapter Four

Blessed are the meek,
for they will inherit the earth.

The so-called 'western' textual tradition, including the familiar
Latin Vulgate Bible, places second in the list of the beatitudes the
one about the meek (Matt. 5:4 or 5). The other manuscripts almost
all insert 'blessed are those who mourn' before it. For the purposes
of our present reflections, I follow the western order; but this is only
for convenience of exposition, and does not involve any claim that
this order is more correct than the other.

The beatitude, 'Blessed are the meek', is an almost exact quotation from Psalm 37, a fact which the evangelist presumably intends
us to notice. The first clue to its meaning, then, must be sought in
the Psalm from which it comes.

The psalmist finds himself in an all too common situation. Looking around the world, he sees all the wrong people prospering. The
people who ought to be doing well, the righteous followers of God's
law, seem to be helpless before the triumphs of the wicked. It does
not make sense. So the psalmist, trying to find comfort if not understanding, meditates on the state of the world in the light of the
mystery of God's purposes.

Do not get heated because of the wicked,
do not be jealous of the perpetrators of sin,
for like the grass they quickly wither,
like fresh green grass they wilt.
Trust in the Lord and do good,
settle down in the land and make faithfulness your friend,
and take great delight in the Lord;

29

rely on him and he will act,
and he will bring forth like daylight your righteousness,
and your right like the noon.
Be silent towards the Lord and supplicate him;
do not get heated because of anyone who makes his way succeed,
or who pulls off his schemes.
Refrain from anger, leave wrath alone,
do not get heated—it would be for nothing but harm!
For the wicked will be cut off,
and those who wait for the Lord,
they are the ones who will inherit the land.
Just a little while and the wicked man does not exist!
However carefully you examine the place, there is no one there!
And the meek will inherit the land,
and they will thoroughly enjoy an abundance of peace.
The wicked man schemes against the righteous
and grinds his teeth at him.
The lord laughs at him,
for he sees his day approaching.   (Ps 37:1–13)

The essential message is clear enough: there is no future for the wicked. And therefore there is no occasion for us to interfere, any more than we have to do anything to make the grass shrivel up in the heat of the sun. Indignation and officiousness are inappropriate reactions. What the Lord does is, simply, laugh. From this point of view, as the psalmist sees it, it is just silly to take the unrighteous seriously. For all their threats and pretensions, there is really nothing to them. To react to them with anger and outrage is to ascribe to them more substance than is their due; and it will achieve nothing but harm. Evil has only so much reality as we give it. We make it more real by reacting to it.

But this does not mean that we can afford to be simplistic about it either. Evil is a part of our world as we know it, and a powerful part at that. It is not for nothing that there is a shift in the tenses in which these first two beatitudes declare their promises: blessed are the poor in spirit, for theirs *is* the kingdom of heaven; blessed are the meek, for they *will* inherit the earth.

The world, seen truly from the point of view of faith, is entirely subject to God's rule. Poverty of spirit clears a way for us to see

30

things in this light, and that begins now. God's rule is not confined to the future.

But God's rule, paradoxically, is, for the duration of this world, inseparable from the rule of the 'Ruler of this world'. And it is only at the end of this world's history that evil will vanish like a bad dream. It is, even now, all in God's hands, so we ought not to get overheated about it. But it is only at the end that we shall see everything put to rights. It is only then that the meek will come into their inheritance.

But it is, precisely, the meek who will inherit the earth. And this is a startling indication of the peculiar way in which God's kingdom operates.

'Meek' is probably not the best way to translate the Greek word used in this beatitude, in fact. And in any case the Greek word matters less here than the Hebrew word used in the underlying verse of Psalm 37: *'anawîm*. This is not primarily a moral word. The *'anawîm* are the underdogs, the people who lack social, political, economic power, the people who are not in a position to control their own circumstances, who cannot pull strings. The people who, on the face of it, stand no chance whatsoever of inheriting the earth.

The Jews, from their bewildering experience of being exiled and then being restored to their own land, but almost at the same time finding that they were not to be restored to a position of political influence, were forced to undertake a radical re-interpretation of the promises made to them by the Lord. It was no longer possible to suppose, in the simple way suggested by the Torah, that material prosperity and power were automatically linked to fidelity to God's commandments. The evidence was all around them that everybody prospered rather than the people of Judah.

This made them sensitive to the element of infidelity in their own life and history: they were afflicted because they had not been faithful to God. A new streak of penitential sadness came into their piety.

But this was not sufficient to account for their historical situation. They came also to suspect that even the most thoroughgoing fidelity to God's way was liable to be combined with poverty and political wretchedness; so they looked for different ways of apprehending the promise which they were still convinced God had made to them. Psalm 37 is part of the process. The important thing is to continue

31

enjoying the Lord, to trust in him and to do good; everything else will fall into place in God's good time. Time, rather than power, is on the side of the righteous.

These two developments to some extent intermingled, producing a peculiar combination of zeal for God's service and a deep pessimism about the possibility of really carrying it out, which at times reaches the point of despair.[1] But out of this grows a renewed sense that even though individuals sin, even though almost the whole people sins, there is within Israel an abiding hope of renewal, because God ensures that the people as a whole never quite falls away. The merits of the fathers outweigh the sins of their descendants, and in any age God sees to it that there is at least one righteous man, for whose sake heaven and earth continue.[2] It is probably in this period that the figure of the *zaddiq* began to emerge, and he is almost certainly the typical exemplar of the hope enshrined in our beatitude.

The *zaddiq* is not necessarily a man who is known to the world; he is likely to be harassed and even persecuted in this world. He may even be killed, like the Maccabean martyrs. But his fidelity makes him, in God's providence, the contact between the world and its Maker's blessing. He is the channel through whom God's mercy flows into the world. And so it is he who ensures the world's survival.[3]

It is to this tradition that our Lord alludes, in all probability, when he tells his disciples that they are the 'salt of the earth' (Matt. 5:13). In slightly more philosophical vein, the Letter to Diognetus calls Christians 'the soul of the world'.[4] The world would go bad and decompose like meat left for too long unsalted and unrefrigerated, it would simply die, were it not for the Christians.

But it is most especially our Lord himself who is the *zaddiq*, and in fact this is a title given to him in the very early church[5]. In him the fumbling hopes of his people come into sharp focus and are fulfilled. He is the Righteous One, who could not be found to save Sodom and Gomorrah (Gen. 18:23ff), but who is now sufficient to save the whole world.

He is the one who was given over into the hands of men, helpless and defenceless before their hatred and their fury, swept away by their triumphant scheming, who yet inherits the earth. Because he was made a little lower than the angels, because he took upon himself the indignity of servitude and the agony of death on a cross, he has been given the name which is above every name, and all authority is given into his hands, in heaven and on earth.

This is the definitive revelation of God's tactic in the world. It is the Crucified One who is engaged in bringing all God's enemies into subjection (cf. 1 Cor 15:24–5). And if our concern is truly for God's kingdom, we must be content that it is so. Our temptation is, and always has been, to try to achieve God's purposes by using the methods of the world. But any such attempt is shut off by the cross of Christ. 'Do not resist the evil' (Matt. 5:39).

And it is in this that we must look for our genuine Christian prudence and practical wisdom. When St Paul says, 'Let the same mind be in you which was in Christ Jesus' (Phil. 2:5), and then goes on with the famous hymn in praise of the abased and exalted Christ, he is not saying to us (as, perhaps, some modern theologians do), 'Of course it is all nonsense, but you must be content with nonsense.' He is offering us Christ as a new pattern of sense, a new way of being sensible. The word he uses (*phroneite*) is the Greek word for 'to be sensible'. This is how Christians are to be sensible. It is therefore legitimate and proper for us to try to see the sense in it, even though we must at the same time recognize that we are, in the last analysis, confronted with the mystery which we cannot fathom of God's infinite and transcendent freedom.

The previous beatitude suggested to us that something had gone wrong with our normal ideas about possession; maybe this beatitude suggests that there is something wrong with our normal ideas about our attempts to do things and get things done. Maybe it is because our ways of trying to achieve things are often inadequate and misconceived that there is a special beatitude for those who find themselves unable to achieve things.

In fact, maybe there is something slightly suspect about the whole idea of 'trying to achieve' something. '*C'est le projet qui m'empêche de vivre*,' as Ionesco complains[6]. Man is made in the image of God and his activity is therefore intended to be in some way reflective of God's activity; and it is not clear that it really makes sense to talk of God 'trying to do something'. 'Whatever the Lord wants, he does' (Ps 135:6). He just does it. He does not try to do it. And there is a world of difference between the two things.

The point here is not just that we cannot think meaningfully of

God wrestling with difficulties and obstacles, though this is, of course, true—for what creature can constitute an obstacle to him who made all creatures? More essentially it is a matter of the way in which God is involved in what he does. He is *wholly* involved. He cannot act in any other way, because he is not such as can be divided. But *trying* to do something inevitably involves a division: it means doing one thing with an eye on something else.

Now obviously in one sense it is unavoidable that we should ourselves act in this way, doing one thing in view of another, and that we should talk of God acting in a similar way. We take medicine in order to get better, we practice scales in order to be able to play the piano. And we can, without total impropriety, say that God became man in order to die and that he died in order to 'redeem our death'. And in at least some of these contexts it is natural enough to speak in terms of 'trying'. We play scales because we are trying to play the piano. And if we can say that God wants all men to be saved, we can probably say that he is trying to save all men.

But there are at least two mistakes we can make with all this kind of thing. First of all, we can forget that the point of doing A for the sake of B is that we hope eventually to be able to do B for the sake of B. We can get into the way of thinking that everything that we do needs some kind of extrinsic justification. Asking 'Why?' can become addictive. We have, by and large, become suspicious of people just doing things because they want to. When all else fails, we resort to curious pseudo-justifications, like going for walks 'for the exercise' or riding a motor bicycle 'for the experience'; worse still, we go all solemn and declare something to be 'important'. So we decorate harmless occupations with high-sounding significances, like taking tea with someone 'just to keep the contact' or 'in case he wants to talk'.

Secondly, we can forget that no amount of trying ever automatically produced the desired result. We take our medicine, but there is always something incalculable about whether or not we get better. We dutifully practise our scales, but some of us become pianists and some of us do not. Between the trying and the doing there is always a discontinuity; the accomplishment always has the quality of a surprise, a gift, an accident.

Both of these mistakes can, I think, help us with our beatitude.

Our concern for purposes and importance is surely a serious way in which we can get out of tune with God. Does it really make sense to say that God 'has a purpose' in what he does? God *is* his own purpose.[7] And in that he is entirely sufficient to himself. And so he cannot be regarded as trying to achieve something in anything like the way in which we try to achieve our objectives. It is a recurrent theme in Meister Eckhart that God acts *ohne Warum*, without a reason why.[8] Strictly speaking, the whole enterprise of creation is quite unnecessary. It is a *jeu d'esprit*, the game that heavenly wisdom plays before God's throne (cf. Prov. 8:30).

And this element of play is, if we care to notice it, deeply stamped on creation. As the German poet and mystic, Angelus Silesius, remarked, 'The rose exists without a reason why; it blossoms because it blossoms' (*Die Ros' ist ohne Warumb, sie blühet weil sie blühet*)[9].

Surely something of the same point is present, too, when our Lord directs us to 'observe the lilies' (Matt. 6:28). They do not toil or spin, they just blossom. We can, if we like, fancifully consider the seed 'wrestling in the ground'[10], but what is a flower for? Even if we insist that flowers play an important part in the whole ecological system, we still have to ask what the whole system is for. The whole world is just a pointless blossoming.

If we are to be and to act like God, if we are to appreciate the act of God, we must come to appreciate the point of pointlessness, the joy of unnecessariness. We must learn to pay due attention to the satisfaction there is sometimes in just doing something for its own sake, and not bias our view of life too much in the direction of those things which are always a struggle and which are always justifiable in terms of some solemn intention.

C. S. Lewis' Screwtape, writing to the young tempter, says:

And now for your blunders. On your own showing you first of all allowed the patient to read a book he really enjoyed, because he enjoyed it and not in order to make clever remarks about it to his new friends. In the second place, you allowed him to walk down to the old mill and have tea there—a walk through country he really likes, and taken alone. . . . Even in things indifferent it is always desirable to substitute the standards of the World, or convention, or fashion, for a human's own real likings and dislikings. I myself would carry this very far. I would make it a rule to eradicate from my patient any strong personal taste which is not actually a sin, even if it is something quite trivial such

35

as fondness for county cricket or collecting stamps or drinking cocoa. Such things, I grant you, have nothing of virtue in them; but there is a sort of innocence and humility and self-forgetfulness about them which I distrust. The man who truly and disinterestedly enjoys any one thing in the world, for its own sake, and without caring twopence what other people say about it, is by that very fact fore-armed against some of our subtlest modes of attack. You should always try to make the patient abandon the people or food or books he really likes in favour of the 'best' people, the 'right' food, the 'important' books. I have known a human defended from strong temptations to social ambition by a still stronger taste for tripe and onions.[11]

Meister Eckhart insists that we must be so united with God that we act from the very ground of our being, which is identical with the ground of his being, so that, like him, we require no further reason why than he does.[12] 'If anyone were to go on asking Life, "Why do you live?", for a thousand years, he would get no other answer (supposing Life could answer) than this: "The reason why I live is that I live". . . . . If anyone were to ask a true man, who acts from his own (inner) ground, "Why do you perform your actions?", if he answers correctly he will say nothing other than this, "I act because I act." '[13]

According to St Thomas, our will is unavoidably set towards the good and can be satisfied only by the totality of goodness in God himself.[14] And this strangely relativizes his doctrine that a human act is an act undertaken for a reason.[15] 'The good' is hardly a reason that we can calculate with, and the totality of good must be far beyond our programming. The ultimate fulfilment of all created being can surely be no other than its final flowering in God from whom it came.

The point can easily be seen by means of a juxtaposition of two apparently similar statements, 'I am going for a walk to fetch the paper'; 'I am going for a walk for the sake of God (or the good).' These two statements patently do not have the same effect. For one thing, the first statement can serve as a reason for going for a walk *rather than* doing something else, such as staying in bed. But the second cannot serve as a reason for doing one thing rather than another, because we are bidden to do *whatever* we do *ad maiorem Dei gloriam.*

This brings us back to our second mistake. If we view life simply

36

in terms of what we can bring about by our own contrivance, we condemn ourselves to a curiously meagre satisfaction. The ultimate goal of everything is God, and God cannot be caught by our scheming. To quote Meister Eckhart again, 'Anyone who looks for God in any particular way, gets the way and lets go of God.'[16] Just as the source of everything is to be situated ultimately in the incalculable spontaneous gift of God, so too its fulfilment depends on him. 'Eye has not seen and ear has not heard and it has not entered the heart of man to conceive what God has made ready for those who love him' (1 Cor. 2:9). The element of discontinuity we sometimes experience between our trying and our achieving is a sign to us of the discontinuity there must be between what we can bring about in this world by our ingenuity and efficiency, and the kingdom of God.

If it is the meek, the helpless, the disabled, who will inherit the earth, this is perhaps because the earth, God's earth, the real earth, can be had on no other terms. It is a gift. Or, in the words of the beatitude, it is an inheritance. And the only achievement required for an inheritance is the achievement of a death. And that means the death of Christ, in whom our old Adam is put to death. It means the death of the whole world order produced by the fantasy, the lie, of sin. 'Let grace come, let this world pass.'[17] The world of sin is the world of calculation, in which effects are exactly proportionate to their immediate cause; it is sin that has 'wages'. But life is a gift, a gift always—as a gift must be—given without thought of arithmetic (Rom. 6:23).

One of the ways in which this commonly impinges on us even in this life is that, when we do achieve something, it is often significantly unlike what we expected to achieve. A preacher or teacher, for instance, is often surprised by his own words and even more surprised by the effect they have on people. His most 'telling' remarks fall flat, and his most unrehearsed and immature thoughts bear fruit. People's lives are changed by casual sayings that they misunderstand or mishear. This is all surely very typical of much that is worth while in our lives. Our own conscious intentions sometimes do little more than provide the comic, but essentially irrelevant, interludes in the drama of our lives.

This ought to open our eyes to an even more basic factor in all our striving. Purposes, such as we can formulate to ourselves, are

37

inevitably limited. We cannot chart any itinerary to the kingdom of God, we can merely plan how to get to London or New York. We may judge that London is on our way to the kindgom of God and we may take steps to get there accordingly, but we may be wrong. Enfolding all our conscious and even unconscious hopes and aspirations, there is the plan of God. and what we, from the point of view of our own limited purposes, regard as failures, may be, from the point of view of God's providence, important steps forward.[18]

It is so simplifying of our lives if we can truly grasp this point. Our disappointments arise because we set our hearts on some particular outcome. But are particular outcomes really worth it? In all that we do, we are a bit like a man planting a tree that he has been given, whose kind he does not know. He may think and hope that it is an apple tree; but he would be ungracious to hold that against it when it produced its first crop of quinces.

It is worth considering how many of the things we do we over-interpret to give ourselves what we feel to be a dignified purpose. For instance, when we are talking to someone, we may think to ourselves, 'I am talking to this person.' That is safe enough. Or we may think, 'I am communicating with this person.' But perhaps he is not paying attention. Or we may think, 'I am giving this person helpful professional advice.' Maybe our advice will turn out to have been unhelpful. We may even, more crudely and ambitiously, think, 'I am helping this person' or 'I am solving all this person's problems.' We may be congratulating ourselves on being just the right counsellor for the person. Before we know where we are, we shall start to think that we are God, running the universe.

But consider how many different developments there might be from the simple fact that I am talking to somebody. It might be my task, in God's providence, to send him to sleep with my well-meant chatter, in which case my carefully chosen words are totally unimportant, and all that matters is that I have a soothing voice. Or it might be my task to give him such bad advice that he goes and talks to somebody else. It might even be my task to annoy him so much that he discovers what a temptation to murder feels like. We know so little of the divine intention in what we do that it is foolish to have more than the most provisional purposes in mind while we do things.

But this surely makes it much more possible for us to act. If heaven and earth depend on what we do next, we shall probably be too scared to do anything. But if nothing depends on what we do next except what we do next, then we can afford to take the risk of doing it.

It is reassuring to realize that any conceivable outcome, whatever it may be, is bound to be within the all-wise providence of God. Nothing at all can come to pass without the will of God.[19] This is the doctrinal foundation for the whole spirituality of self-abandonment to divine providence, associated particularly with the name of the Jesuit, de Caussade, but taught with almost as much insistence by Julian of Norwich before him, and Thérèse of Lisieux after him[20] and by so many others that it can safely be accepted as an integral part of Christian tradition.[21] Whatever actually happens, precisely as such, has to be regarded as the act of God, whatever other comments on it we may wish to make.

If this is taken seriously, it is impossible to regard anything at all that happens in this world as simply disastrous.[22] Disaster is always disaster relative to some particular hope or desire; no disaster within our life in this world can be, simply, disaster from the point of view of eternal life and bliss. On the other hand, no success within this world can be regarded as simply success from the point of view of eternal life, because it always remains possible that we shall bungle our death. But this sobering reflection needs to be kept in a proper perspective. God's purpose is our salvation; we should not think of him maliciously trying to catch us out, waiting, as it were, to catch us off our guard and pounce on us when we are in sin.[23] All his works are for the making of man,[24] not for his undoing. And so it is more fundamental to a truly theological view of life to be hopeful than to be anxious. Even things that go wrong are within the overall process whereby God leads us to himself. After all, the epitome of all sin and all disaster, the murder of the Son of God, is the very centre of all hope. That is the way in which God takes our sin and our suffering into account, and that is how we, too, must take it into account.

Julian of Norwich boldly teaches that sin, from the point of view of eternity, will be no shame to man, 'but rather worship'. As she sees it, with profound theological acumen, sin 'has no manner of being', and can be known only in the pain which attends it. Sin enters into reality, into the scheme of things, only because Christ suffers all our pain.[25] Apart from that, it is a nonsense and cannot be fitted into any overall picture of reality. It cannot be taken into account. Any anxious concern to defend ourselves against it is to ascribe to it more substance than it possesses.

In the early decades of the second Christian century, this lesson was taught in a different way to that strange Roman visionary, Hermas. In a vision he was instructed to stop harping on his sins in his penitential prayer, and to pray positively about righteousness.[26]

Evil is indeed an impressive element in our world; but that is only because our world is lacking in authentic substance. It is God's will that is the proper measure of reality; and that is expressed in Christ, who is his Will. And in him there is no sin, and all that could be described as evil is transmuted into glory.

We are faced, then, with a double temptation. There is the temptation to suppose that the resurrection has already taken place (2 Tim. 2:18), that, if we could only see it, this world already *is* paradise. But the full inheritance of the earth is still to come, and when it comes it will come plainly. 'When Christ who is our life is revealed, then you too will be revealed with him' (Col. 3:4). The régime of paradise is not a régime of hiddenness.

But there is also the temptation to suppose that what we see all around us is the last word of reality. It is not. With the eye of faith we must, like Moses, be as if we saw what is not seen (cf. Hebr. 11:27). And it is what is not seen that grounds in reality all that is seen (Hebr. 11:3). And that grounding in reality covers what we call evil only by absorbing it into good. In the great theological vision of Julian of Norwich, 'all shall be well' is rooted in 'all is well'. It is the eternal, unchanging gaze of God's love that establishes what is, most deeply, true: and in that gaze, all is well.[27] When that appears, we shall know—what we cannot at present grasp except by faith—that 'all shall be well', too, has been fulfilled.

But this, of course, means that we cannot in any finally serious sense break our world and our experience of life down into two separate categories: success and failure. It is in whatever is the case that we must yield ourselves to the creative, redemptive act of God.

This obviously does not exclude the possibility of our doing much that changes the world around us. That may well be a frequent consequence of our yielding ourselves to the act of God. But it does mean that we are required to take very seriously the gap between our efforts and any genuine achievement. Whatever we achieve in this life is itself only a kind of raw material, or perhaps a symbolic sketch of beatitude. We should therefore, as the *Bhagavad Gita* says, act with detachment from the results of action.[28] What is important is what we are doing, not what we are trying to do.

Before she died, St Thérèse of Lisieux said:

> I scatter to right and to left the good seed that the good God puts into my little hand for my little birds. What happens then is its own business. I do not concern myself with that at all. . . . The good God says to me, 'Give, give, always give, without bothering yourself at all about the results.'[29]

If we can take all of this to heart, then we shall begin to find mildly ridiculous a whole approach to life that might otherwise have been attractive. From this perspective, it seems rather silly to be too preoccupied with getting ourselves into a strong position to get things done, with being able and influential enough to change the course of events. However powerful we are, the most we can do is change the décor of a world that is still collapsing into its own death. The new heaven and new earth will be created by God in such a way that they gloriously fulfil all that has been adumbrated in this present world, but most emphatically they will not be created by this present world.

It is what we are doing, whatever it may be, that is, in some inscrutable way, in union with the act of God, pertinent to the final disclosure of God's world. What we are actually doing, not what we think we are doing or what we are aiming at or trying to do. The essential thing, then, is not to strain to realize our objectives, but to do whatever we do, and do it, so to speak, into the providence of God.

And that, surely, is at least part of the 'meekness' of which our beatitude speaks. It is the moral, spiritual attitude which is learned from helplessness as a particular human condition, but which generalizes into a name for the human condition as such. And the beatitude invites us to acknowledge that it is a good and happy thing that it is so.

41

Chapter Five

'Nothing that appears is good,' declares St Ignatius of Antioch, possibly quoting a contemporary proverb; and he goes on to cap it with the paradoxical remark, 'Our God, Jesus Christ, being in the Father (i.e. having disappeared from our world), appears all the more.'[1] It is in his disappearance from the world that Christ really comes into his own; his universal lordship is linked with his ascension, which is his disappearance from the world.[2]

Origen also knows Ignatius' proverb, and he quotes it in connexion with our Lord's instruction about prayer: 'Go into your room and shut the door' (Matt. 6:6),[3] and this probably gives us the proper interpretation of the proverb. We should not pray *showily*. God does not work *showily*.

In fact there is a long tradition behind St Ignatius and after him in Greek thought, that it is characteristic of God to work quietly, without a fuss.[4] God acts from the fullness of his being, and so does not have to bluster.

Is not this another facet of that elusive quality of meekness to which our beatitude directs our attention? All our jockeying for position, striving to get ourselves into a more influential and powerful place, is the bluster which comes from relative emptiness. This is perhaps one of the most typical differences between simply doing something and trying to do something: the one comes from fullness, the other from deficiency.

It was, as usual, a very real insight that led to the Gnostic characterization of this world of our everyday experience as *hysterêma*, 'deficiency', over against God's world of *plerôma*, 'fullness'. And deficiency, in desperation, seeks to overcome its own incompleteness, but has not got the resources with which to do so. This is the source of its agonized blundering around, busily achieving insubstantial results.[5]

Our beatitude of the meek is a call to us to abandon the kind of activism which belongs to *hysterêma*, and to live rather by the quietness, the unshowiness, the unobtrusiveness, of God; to be silent and suppliant before him.

Measured by the world's standards of impressiveness, God must always finally be found wanting. The world judges impressiveness comparatively, but God is not part of that kind of competition. God cannot be compared. This does not just mean that he is so far ahead of his competitors that comparison is a waste of time; it means, quite strictly, that he cannot be compared, he does not enter into comparison. If we insist on the competitive terms of our world, God is a non-starter.

And he must be so. God is not a part of our world, he is not a part of reality. Any revelation of himself within the world is always at the same time a distortion, because it makes it look as if he were this rather than that, here rather than there; it makes him particular. But he is not particular. That is why he always takes steps to contradict his own appearances in one way or another.

Thus, for instance, a magnificent theophany is laid on at Sinai, with thunder and smoke and trumpet blast—the full works (Exod. 19:16ff). This is how we should expect God to display himself. But when he does it again for the benefit of Elijah, he is careful to disclose that he is not in the earthquake or the mighty wind. It is almost as if he were deliberately re-creating the kind of theophany that had so impressed the people at Sinai, in order to emphasize that he is not simply identical with that kind of manifestation, though he can use it as one way of revealing himself. Elijah is the appointed witness to the fact that the manifestation is also a distortion. For him, the Lord was not in all the impressive, noisy things; the Lord came after, in a thin little whispering noise (the sound of a thin *d'mamah*, translated 'whisper', but etymologically connected with the word for 'silence' which is used in Psalm 37:7) (1 Kings 19:11ff).

Even the appearing of God in the incarnation has a principle of disappearance built into it. The final move, so to speak, is heralded by the announcement, 'It is in your interest that I should go away' (John 16:7). And this enfolds both the disappearance in the passion and the element of disappearance which runs through all the resurrection stories, culminating in the ascension. Origen has good reason to say that Christ 'was sent, not only to become known, but also to remain hidden.'[6]

God cannot finally be revealed in any particular within our world, because he cannot be confined within any particular. God is never this *rather than* that, here *rather than* there.[7]

The meekness of the beatitude is a response to this radical impossibility of comparison and competitiveness in God. It learns to reverence this principle of God's own act, and comes in turn to live like that itself. It lets go of the besetting need to get or to do or to be this rather than that. It becomes content just to be whatever this or that it may turn out to be at any given moment. It drops the bluster of trying to achieve something, trying to conquer life, trying to put everything straight. Its acts come simply from what it is, from a fullness of being which is an echo of, and indeed a participation in, the fullness of God's being.

But this renunciation of competitiveness is costly. The model for us is Christ on the cross. And the sense of it is better explored with the help of some of the great figures of tragic literature than by any sentimental optimism of nature worship. Take Agamemnon, for instance, or Oedipus or Hamlet. They are men who are trapped. Facing his terrible choice at Aulis, Agamemnon wonders, 'Which of these is without evil?' He has to 'put on the yoke of necessity'.[8]

That is often the way it is in life. Life in this world is a trap. Over and over again we find ourselves in situations which constrain us, and there is no true escape. We daydream of ideal choices, but we have to live with and in the trap. We are trapped in working conditions or personal relationships which bring out the worst in us, we are trapped in the consequences of our own or others' past misdeeds or follies, we are trapped in the social and economic systems in which we live. We have only the mammon of unrighteousness with which to invest for eternal life (cf. Luke 16:9).

The resulting sense of powerlessness is one of the major psychological pains of our time,[9] and it can easily lead us to despair.

The answer that the gospel gives us is an austere one, but it is surely the only fully realistic answer that there is. It tells us that it is only by accepting the trap that we can hope to change anything. It is not by fretting and flapping, but by bearing the cross of our helplessness and frustration, in union with Christ bearing his cross, that we shall find any genuine power for a more satisfying life.

We may feel an agony of futility over our seemingly total unimportance, convinced that all that we do and say and are makes no difference at all to anybody or anything; we may long just to break out violently and destructively, simply to assert that we are real and that we do make a difference. But that would only add to the bluster of the world of deficiency, *hysterêma*. Instead, our lack must be accepted as the very locus of God's act. It is a sacrament of his unobtrusive presence. Meekness receives that sacrament.

And its reward, its hoped-for end, is the earth. And this should not be unduly spiritualized. It is the earth that is vandalized by our sinfulness and pride, and it is the earth that is to be redeemed by God's act.[10] His promise contains a new earth as well as a new heaven. If our hearts bleed at the thought and the sight of what we are doing to our world, we should take comfort at this: though we are powerless to do much to avert its ruin, we can be meek in God and wait until the blustering storms of this world of fantasy are over. The seed of the new earth is the man who is meek, the faithful, helpless one, the *zaddiq*, whose schemes do not prosper, but who does not despair even in death, even in the death of the whole world. What is real is the world of God's creating, not the world of deficiency. Just a moment, and then we shall not be able to find a trace of the violence and wickedness which seemed so impressive— not even if we go hunting with a microscope. It is God's world that is real and does not wilt, and it is into his world that man is put, to enjoy with God for ever the blessed contemplation of all that is.

Blessed are those who are not in too much of a hurry to get things done, and know how to wait, helpless, nailed to their cross. Against all the odds, it is truly they who will inherit the earth.

And perhaps it is only they who could inherit the earth. It depends on what kind of inheritance we envisage. Surely the proper inheritance is for us once again to become Adam, and that we can only do in Christ, the new Adam. And it is interesting to see how the new Adam is presented in St John's gospel: there, the first resurrection story is clearly intended to be a harking back to the story of creation. There is a man and a woman in a garden. And the man is the gardener, Mary is quite right about that. He is the new gardener in the new paradise. And what happens in this new

45

paradise? Exactly what happened in the first one: a naming. Just as Adam named the beasts, so Christ names Mary. And it is when he names her that she understands and recognizes him (John 20:11f).

Since the fall, our human lordship has been exercised chiefly in exploitation and manipulation. But the essential lordship of Adam is seen in naming. According to St Ephrem, Adam, in naming the animals, is truly sharing in God's creativity.[11] In Christ we, who share in his Holy Spirit, become once more the namers in his world, and as such help each creature into the fullness of its own being.[12]

So, if we are to inherit the earth, we must learn to recognize, to name, to liberate things into themselves, instead of constantly trying to organize things and make something of them for ourselves.

And this is something we must do for one another, too. It is a pity that we have come to think so much in terms of helping people to solve their problems. Almost inevitably this leads us to think in terms of diagnosing their problems, and diagnosis means fitting their unique situations to clinical abstractions. It involves naming only in the sense of finding the appropriate ready-made label.

But the way of Adam is not to diagnose, not to fit things to ready-made labels, it is to recognize, or better, to cognize (because Adam's knowing is a knowing for the first time, it is the aboriginal human knowing, the first and immediate derivative from God's own creative knowing); it is to cognize each creature, each situation, in its uniqueness, in its own unique way of expressing the likeness of God.

It is when we are finally stumped, when we can think of nothing more that we can do, that we can most easily—though even then it is not, simply, easy—appreciate that problems are not just things calling for solutions. A problem is, more essentially, a unique situation calling for expression. It calls for a poet, a painter, a composer. And sometimes, in God's providence, we may be that poet or painter or composer. Each individual situation in our world is an artistic, rather than an administrative, challenge.[13] If we would inherit the earth, it must be, not by competent administration, but by something much more like artistic sensitivity and creativity.

It is surely the meek, those whose instinct is not to rush out and do something, but rather to look, helpless, passive before reality, and then, in union with God's Word, to be, to speak, the word which releases each creature into itself, it is they who can enjoy a proper lordship in the earth. So do not get heated because of the wicked, there is no future in them or in your fury. Rather rejoice hugely in the Lord and be content to rest in his truthfulness and to gaze with wonder upon the world of his making, and, with the eye of faith and hope, to see that world in the making even in the despair and helplessness of the world of everyday experience.

C INTERLUDE

Chapter Six

The first two beatitudes that we have considered, the beatitudes of the poor and the meek and helpless, seem rather negative in their import: they are concerned to hold back the flood-tide of possessiveness and activism. The effect of them is to indicate a kind of spaciousness, even a kind of emptiness. It is in this emptiness that there is room for God to be king, and for him to create the world of his devising. It is in this emptiness that there is room for us to be remade.

The heart of our remaking must, of course, be charity. This is the virtue which divinizes and makes perfect. But charity, in this life, cannot flourish without the other two theological virtues of faith and hope. And in a way our first two beatitudes are concerned with faith and hope, setting up the space for charity, whose symptoms the remaining beatitudes describe.

Like the first two beatitudes, faith and hope, too, have something negative about them. They are 'antidote' virtues. They free us from the tyranny of immediacy. Faith enables us to see things from the point of view of God's truth, so that we can resist the pressures brought to bear on us by 'things seen' (cf. 2 Cor. 4:18). And hope encourages us to be patient as God works out his purpose in his own way, freeing us from the obsessive need to get results right away, and from the prudential concern always to know how results are going to be achieved. And they lead us out of the world which is ruled by human fantasy (or worse), into the real, but hidden, world of God's making, the world which does not yet exist publicly (which is why hope is so essential), but which is utterly guaranteed by God's intention. Living by faith and hope, then, means living in a kind of emptiness, within which God is creating, but in which, as yet, there is nothing except raw material and fleeting images. All that is seen derives what substantiality it has from what is not seen (cf. Hebr. 11:3), both in the sense that it is real only in so far as it corresponds to the will of him whom no man can see, and in the sense that it will achieve its own full reality only in the new world which is not yet revealed to be seen.

If we read the first chapters of Genesis as prophetic, rather than historical—and we shall be by no means the first to do so[1]—we must surely situate ourselves essentially right at the beginning of the story. 'The earth was formlessness and emptiness.' We are in, and we are part of, that primordial chaos, over which God's Spirit broods like a mother bird hatching her eggs (Gen. 1:2). The full imprint of the creative Word, which brings things into their own actuality, is still, from our point of view, in the future. The Word of God is even now establishing his rule over the world, but it is only at the end, when the final enemy, the dragon of the deep, the monster death, has been defeated, that the kingdom will be accomplished and the whole world will be subjected to the Father through the kingly rule of his Word (cf. 1 Cor. 15:24–8).

Our world, then, is a world of deficiency, not a world of fullness. But it is also a world of deception.[2] However we care to tell the story, our world as we have it now is a world in whose beginnings sin must be included. We have fallen, we are not in paradise. This world of ours is the world of our fall.[3] It is not merely a world of deficiency in the sense that it is an unfinished world, it is a world of deficiency also in the sense that it is defective, a world that has gone wrong.

And a key element in its wrongness is its attempt to appropriate itself to itself, its attempt to make itself independent of God's making. It clutches at its unfinishedness and tries to find perfection there. Its deficiency is accepted as if it were completeness. In the terms of the old myth, man grasped at a knowledge for which neither he nor the world was yet prepared. And so he 'knows' what is not there to be known. His 'knowledge' is a fraud and brings him under the sway only of the 'Father of lying' (cf. John 8:44).

This is why the antidote virtues are so necessary. Man must learn to see by another light than that of his pretended 'knowledge', and he must learn to wait for a fulfilment that is not yet given.

And in this way he must learn to be, precisely, incomplete,

49

deficiency. He must learn to be a space within which God can be known to act.

This is the emptiness, the void, that is taken by God and shaped into his new creation. But if he is to shape it, we must beware of trying to impose our own shape on it. Until the finished product is disclosed, there must remain a kind of shapelessness. Indeed, in some sense, perhaps we must say that there must always be a kind of shapelessness, or at least something that we can best apprehend as shapelessness. If man is being made in God's image and likeness, man must be prepared to find himself as elusive and unfathomable as God himself is. And so man must resist the temptation to clutter up the emptiness created by faith and hope.

This is the importance of the Thomistic doctrine that we can never know, directly, the essence of our own soul. The final 'what-ness' of our own identity escapes us.[4] And so we can never know whether we are 'being ourselves', or not with any absolute certainty. And, since it is in the essence of the soul that grace works, according to St Thomas,[5] a consequence of this is that we can never be absolutely sure that we are in a state of grace, or that any particular eventuality in our lives is a product of grace, rather than a continu-ing sign of the primordial chaos or the original sin. There is an ambiguity about all that occurs in our lives, which we must not seek to resolve. It is the ambiguity which obliges us to keep on acknowledging that we are God's handiwork, not our own. Since we cannot even monitor what he is doing with any degree of accu-racy, there is nothing left for us except to abandon ourselves to his activity, accepting that all our plans and works are ambiguous as to whether or not they are significant for our ultimate fulfilment.

On the other hand, mere emptiness is not enough either. We are even now being shaped for eternity, and this shaping must produce effects even now. Mere emptiness, according to our Lord's parable, is just an invitation to seven devils worse than the first to move in on us (cf. Matt. 12:43–5).

What is needed, then, is some way of ensuring that the emptiness is not left merely vacant, which will at the same time ensure that the fullness is genuine, and that means genuinely open to the mys-tery, the elusiveness, the unfinishedness, of God's act in creating and remaking.

50

We need something that will give shape to the spaciousness without losing the positive mystery inherent in the shapelessness.

Clearly enough the answer to our puzzle must be something to do with faith, hope and charity. It is charity that gives shape, and faith and hope prevent that shape from closing in prematurely upon itself, taking false possession of itself and so blocking off the perfecting work of God. But can we say anything more than this?

At least we can indicate how our present puzzle has a certain kinship with other puzzles. If 'God is love' (1 John 4:8), we should not be surprised to find that there is a certain affinity between the way in which charity gives shape without ever simply becoming shape, and the way in which God discloses himself without ever losing his mysteriousness. Charity gives shape to all our lives, it informs all true virtues and so shows itself in a myriad of different ways; but what is charity in itself? St Paul, in his famous chapter on love (1 Cor. 13), seems to indicate that any conceivable manifestation of charity is, in itself, ambiguous. We can practise heroic generosity and still be 'without love'. Similarly the God who is seen, above all in Jesus Christ, is still the God whom 'no one has seen or can see' (1 Tim. 6:16). The Word of God is precisely the Word in which we hear the silence of God.[6] The Son of God is the visibility of the Father, but only in such a way that the Father is the invisibility of the Son.[7] The visibility does not cancel out the invisibility.

Faith, then, as a response to God's truth and God's revelation, must always respect the hiddenness that there is even in revelation. The living God is not an idol, and this means that he cannot be identified as any 'thing' within reality. He is 'no thing'. But yet he gives himself and he desires to be known. It is faith that responds to God's imparting of himself by seeking always the Unseen who is making himself seen, not idolizing whatever visibility he may give himself. So faith preserves the space within which God can act as the totally free author of all things, ensuring that he is not reduced in our minds to being simply a part of our world.

Consider also how essential hope is to any real love, even love between human beings. In marriage, for instance, two people pledge themselves to each other. But what is it that they are giving each other? If we say that they are giving themselves, what does that mean? Does either one so fully possess himself or herself that he or she can simply give it to another? In giving oneself, one is giving what does not even exist. A commitment of oneself to another 'for better, for worse', is a commitment of one knows not what to one knows not what. We simply do not know what we shall be even in a few hours' time, let alone after years or decades. Yet clearly such commitment of one's unknown future is a recognized and desired feature of love. Even where there is no formal commitment, some implicit pledge of loyalty is surely taken to be indispensable. And such a commitment gives shape, in one sense, to a life, but cannot possibly be taken as pre-empting the issue of what will be. To give oneself to another human being, in marriage or in friendship, or to pledge oneself to the service of God in baptism or in religious vows, is to make an act of hope; otherwise it is total nonsense. Where love is offered and accepted in any other spirit, it can only last by the most unlikely fluke. It is probable that one of the reasons why marriage has become such an unstable institution in our society is that people are presuming too much on what they know and feel in the present, and identify that with their love. They do not face stoutly enough the element of mystery and unknownness that there has to be in such an enterprise.

All of this can, perhaps, help us to appreciate a bit more clearly the importance of the principle of maintaining the mystery while avoiding sheer vacuity. But it still does not really solve our problem, of how we can actually set about such a paradoxical task. It is charity, with faith and hope, that must structure our void, so much is clear; but, it seems, charity itself must always be ambiguous in all its manifestations, and so it, too, has to be kept as a kind of void. Its signs and symptoms may be important, but they must never be latched on to. As George Macdonald remarks, 'You *cannot* perfectly distinguish between the true and the false while you are not yet quite dead; neither indeed will you when you are quite dead—that is, quite alive, for then the false will never present itself.'[8] Discernment becomes possible only when it is no longer called for. So long as we are in this world, in which the ambiguity remains, we shall never be able to diagnose with full confidence the roots and motives from which our ideas and actions come.

In all this welter of ambiguity, however, there is one provision which God has made for us which does provide a kind of bridge over the abyss, a kind of framework in which we can be formed in the fullness of charity with at any rate less than usual risk of trivialization. And that is the provision of ritual signs and symbols.

In paradise there was no temple, and in the new creation there will be no temple, because in each case the totality is known to be the place where God is worshipped. But in between, in this world of sin, God appoints a particular altar, a particular holy place, a particular sacred act, in which we can worship him. Different stages in the history of redemption have different temples, but so long as we are in this world, some kind of temple is needed, and it is a false spirituality which spurns it.[9]

Love must use signs, it must express itself in some kind of symbol; and the signs that simply appear spontaneously, from ourselves, are all ambiguous and so cannot be trusted, in themselves, to form and foster true charity in us. We must be formed by something that expresses for us the mystery of God and the mystery of his love, which is the heart of all love and of all worship. But it must do so in a way that does not violate the shapelessness, the spaciousness, of the mystery of faith and hope. And surely this is precisely what the sacraments and, to a lesser degree, the sacramentals, the whole ritual structure of the church, in fact, is intended to provide for us.

We have become so used to psychologizing everything, that it is perhaps unusually difficult for our present age to accept the value of ritual symbols. Ritual can easily incur the charge of 'inauthenticity'; it does not seem to express *us*. We turn instinctively to more immediately expressive and 'relevant' gestures and modes of behaviour.

But is there not a danger that we are being very short-sighted in our depreciation of ritual? Can we really measure 'authenticity' simply against our conscious mental and volitional state? Is ritual in any case intended to express what we happen to be thinking or feeling? Is there not something more basic and objective than that, which needs to be expressed?

We often use the word 'superficial' in a derogatory sense, but this is very unfair to surfaces (and 'superficial' means 'to do with surfaces', from the Latin *superficies*). Do we necessarily see things more truly if we peel off their surface? Can a surface not be precisely the way the reality of a thing is meant to become apparent?[10]

A great deal of the trouble comes from the feeling that somewhere underneath, out of sight, is the 'real thing', or more likely the 'real me'. This device allows us to ignore what is actually open to our inspection, in favour of something that is, *ex hypothesi*, hidden. In itself this is not necessarily a bad thing, because there is indeed a mystery at the heart of all created being. But this mystery belongs to God and is not open to our scrutiny. The trouble begins when we suppose that we have some privileged access to our own 'inside', which allows us to 'interpret' to our own advantage the gap there is between inside and outside. A similar ploy allows us to be sceptical about what other people appear to be; we assume that somehow we can get at what they 'really' are underneath, and that this entitles us to disregard what they appear to be on the surface, often to their considerable disadvantage.

But this is a highly dangerous approach to life. To some extent, obviously, we can estimate what people are feeling and thinking, and even what their subconscious motives may be, independently of what a casual observer might be able to see. But once we raise the question of what is underneath the surface, we ought to go very much further than we generally do.

A favourite slogan in recent times has been, 'It is not what you do that matters, it is what you are.' In one sense, this may be true; what we are in God is of ultimate significance. But what we are in God is not yet in any simple sense a fact about us. It is certainly not a fact that can be ascertained by ourselves or by anyone else, even by the most sophisticated methods of probing the depths of a human person. But apart from that, what we are is not of any special interest. What we do may be far more important, because what we do may actually be far more expressive of the ultimate truth of what we are in God, than what we, as a matter of contingent fact, happen to 'be' independently of what we are doing. We can, for instance, have a keen dislike of someone and an informed disapproval of him too; yet we can do him a favour. Why should we be more interested in our dislike and disapproval of him than in the stupendous fact that we can do something charitable which does not simply express what we 'are' in ourselves?

What we do can be very much more versatile and worth while than what goes on behind the scenes in our psychological life. And it may be of greater significance for our being in God, because it may express his true purpose, even while it does not express anything we could clearly call our own purpose. We sometimes say, 'I don't know why I did it,' of some deed which has surprised us.

In the same way ritual behaviour can be expressive of a profundity of truth which transcends the capacity of our normal psychological awareness and powers. Ritual can express things which are true in God, but which are more basic than anything 'we' could express for ourselves; they can express a charity which is beyond the capacity of our complex and muddled motives and intentions. The 'inner' man who is, according to St Paul, being renewed day by day in the Holy Spirit, does not refer to our 'soul', over against our body, nor does it refer to any part of ourselves which we might conceivably discover by some process of investigation or introversion. The 'outer' man who is dying, inch by inch, includes all our psychological faculties (cf. 2 Cor. 4:16). It is body and soul that are heading for death, and it is body and soul that are being renewed by the Holy Spirit. But often it is the body which comes first (cf. Rom. 12:1), precisely because of our ability to express in deed what we are not yet capable of apprehending in our minds or in our wills.

One of the ways in which the church has sought to assist the growth of the 'new man' in us, is by the practice of religious obedience, by which, to some extent at least, a man's deeds are detached from his inner life and governed externally. This breaks the short-circuit and allows for a person's behaviour to express charity, the indwelling of the Holy Spirit, instead of just his own ideas and fancies.

But the most basic way, which is offered to all Christians, is the way of ritual, the way of all the sacramental signs and symbols in which the church structures her essential life.

The church's sacramental life is a kind of sacred drama in which we can act out symbolically our identity as the church, the bride of Christ 'without spot or wrinkle' (Eph. 5:27), in spite of the fact that, in ourselves, we are covered in spots and wrinkles. It is a chance for us to enter into something bigger than ourselves, and so strengthen the new creation which is germinating within us, without too much risk that we shall try to misappropriate it as we did our first creation.

It should not dismay us that we do not always find it 'meaningful' or 'relevant', that sometimes it does not 'speak to us' or 'do anything

55

for us'; we should not complain that our sharing in it seems 'empty' or 'inauthentic'. It is essentially we who have to become adapted to the liturgy, not the other way round. It is the food of grown ups.[11] Of course this is unusually tricky at a time of rapid liturgical change and experimentation like our own; the church is trying out liturgies, and—we may devoutly hope—will discard many of the strange practices and texts, especially vernacular texts, with which we are currently afflicted. But even now, as the essential thing is, after all, not the intellectual or artistic value of the texts, but the whole event, the doing, of the liturgy, we ought to try to yield ourselves to it, playing our part within it, as being something authentic in itself, inviting us into its authenticity, not needing to derive authenticity from us. If it is not always 'meaningful', this may be because we are not yet mature enough in our new creation to appreciate its meaning. If it does not speak to us, that may be because we are still deaf and uneducated in certain ways. If our participation feels 'empty', that may be because we have not yet filled our role in the new manhood with much understanding. St Paul tells us to 'put on Christ' (Rom. 13:14). Perhaps we can say that in the liturgy we 'dress up in Christ'. It is a pretence, like all dressing up, like all acting; but in this case it is a pretence which is the best formation we are going to get for the eventual reality of what we can only do now in symbols and ritual gestures.

Precisely because this drama of the church's life does not concern itself particularly with what is going on in you or me individually, it resists any attempt that the old Adam may make to misappropriate it to himself. Of course liturgy can become a fad, a personal hobby, an obsession; but it can surely do so only when we stop treating it as liturgy, that is, a public task in which we are given an objective role to play.

And so the rituals of the church can structure the space created by faith and hope, by poverty and meekness, without violating its emptiness, and without abandoning us to the risk of mere emptiness.

If we entrust ourselves faithfully and with perseverance and generosity to the ritual, symbolic expressions of charity which the church provides for us, they will surely give us the context in which the more spontaneous signs of charity can also be trusted. If the liturgy, with the eucharist at its centre, is the source and high point of our whole Christian life,[12] the other signs of charity which well

56

up spontaneously from the spaciousness of faith and hope must be reckoned to derive from the eucharist and to find their fulfilment in it. It is not they that measure the worthwhileness of our participation in the liturgy, but the other way round. The spontaneous signs are all of them ambiguous; it is the ritual signs which are unambiguous. It is the ritual signs which cherish the root of charity, the new man, in us; and it is our fidelity to the ritual which encourages us to hope that our spontaneous expressions are truly coming to be more simply expressions of charity, with less admixture of the old Adam.

It is against this background, then, that we can now turn to the remaining beatitudes, which all draw our attention to different symbols, or signals, of charity. They must never fill the emptiness of poverty and helplessness in such a way that the emptiness of faith and hope changes to the false security of possession and achievement. It is in their insertion into the church's drama, and especially the eucharist, that they are purged of their narrowness so that they can indeed serve the mystery of unbounded, and therefore incomprehensible, love.

D SYMPTOMS OF CHARITY

Chapter Seven

Blessed are those who mourn,
for they will be comforted.

The first two beatitudes we have considered establish a kind of
emptiness: the letting go of possessiveness and of go-getting activism
should create space for other motives to come into play but, by
themselves, they could just leave a void. The remaining beatitudes,
in different ways, warn us off leaving a void.

'Blessed are those who mourn' warns us off a purely negative
kind of detachment and helplessness, which would say 'I have
nothing and can do nothing, but what the Hell! I don't care.' Those
who do not care do not mourn, and so are not in the way of the
beatitudes. Blessedness is declared to be upon those who are not
only poor and meek, but also mourners. This rules out any state of
numbed emotional apathy.

This ought to remind us that emotion, responsiveness, is part of
what human beings are meant to be. Some kinds of spirituality
seem to inculcate such a systematic distrust of spontaneous human
reactions as to suggest that the ideal is a rock-like condition in
which we feel nothing, and act in a mechanical way simply in
accordance with abstract principles. But Ezekiel's prophecy stands
firmly against any such programme: 'I shall remove the heart of
stone from your flesh and put into you a heart of flesh' (36:26). It
is part of our fallenness to be hard-hearted and incapable of warm
responses, whether positive or negative. It is a part of our redemption to become more able to react.

This is obviously not to say that we ought always to be as
emotional as possible, or that we ought to give free expression to
every emotion that occurs to us. A certain discipline in our emotions

and in our expression of them is no bad thing. But it should be a discipline that is truly *in* our emotions, not just against them.

It is helpful to clarify just what goes wrong with our emotions; then we shall see more clearly what is involved in their redemption.

One very evident disease of our emotions is that they get out of step with their supposed objects. We do not then react simply to what is there and we do not react proportionately to what is there; our emotions take on an independent life of their own, attaching themselves more or less at random to the various actual circumstances and events of our lives. In so far as our emotions have become self-generating, only tangentially related to their supposed stimuli, a major part of their redemption will consist in making them more authentically responsive.

What is wrong with our emotions, in such a case, is not that they are emotional, not even that they are too emotional. It is that—however hectic may be the feelings they produce—they are not really 'emotion' at all, because they are not *moved* by anything. And this is why they are so patently out of step with a clear-headed rational response to the situation. The answer is not for them to be brought under tyrannical rational control, but for them to become truly 'emotional' (moved), in becoming in themselves reasonable, a sound response to something that is actually there, a reaction which corresponds to what we know with our minds to be the truth of the situation.

It is important not to misunderstand this idea of rational, disciplined emotions, because another important disease of our emotions is precisely that they can come to be suppressed or manipulated in a cold and calculating fashion.

It is easy enough to see how such a disease arises. Our spontaneous emotions, even when they are not disordered, are likely to be upsetting. Fierce emotions, even if they are appropriate, disrupt our lives and make us vulnerable to all manner of things we cannot control. We feel much safer if we are not at the mercy of life in this way. Accordingly we take steps to make ourselves less sensitive; we either try to do without emotions entirely, or we try to deflect our emotions into approved channels, which means, in effect, trying to pretend that we do not have some of the emotions that we do in fact have, and that we do have some that we do not in fact have.

To what extent we can actually deceive ourselves about our own emotions is, perhaps, a moot point. But there is no doubt that we can get ourselves into a state in which very little genuine emotion reaches our consciousness at all. What is more, there is some reason to believe that in our own age there is considerable social pressure on us to push us in just such a direction. The risk of authentic emotion is not one that is socially endorsed; on the other hand, the cultivation of spurious emotion is all too obvious a part of our world.

Whatever else our beatitude may mean, it is quite certainly an apologia for authentic emotional responses. And as such it contradicts any spirituality or presentation of the gospel which seeks to eliminate or to falsify our emotions.

And one such presentation of the gospel is the insistence on Christian 'joy' at all costs. Our beatitude not only vindicates emotion, it specifically vindicates negative emotion. Whatever we are to make of texts like 'Rejoice in the Lord always' (Phil. 4:4), they are most emphatically not a ban on feeling miserable. *Blessed* are those who feel miserable.

At the very least our beatitude comes to support us when we are unhappy, and to defend us against all bossy attempts to oblige us to be cheered up. And St Paul himself confirms this, with his command to weep with those who weep. He does not say, 'Cheer up those who weep,' but 'Weep with those who weep' (Rom. 12:15).

It is worth reflecting on the very ambiguous motives which may underlie the compulsion towards Christian 'joy'. In many ways, no doubt, it is well meant, when we try to cheer people up and even when we try to convince them on grounds of faith that they ought to be less despondent. But can we honestly say that that is all there is to it? Are we not ourselves rather selfishly relieved when people do cheer up, for instance? After all, they are a bore with all their misery, they embarrass us with all their emotion, they perplex us with their pain. People who insist on being miserable or sick, people who even take it upon themselves to die, are breaking one of the most rigid taboos our society has set up. Is it not all too probable that the insistence on Christian 'joy' is, to a considerable extent, only a pious version of the social pressure on us not to be weak and ailing? And if this is so, the rule of cheerfulness is but another instance of the way in which fallen man disowns his true emotions,

60

and allows only selected, programmed, surrogate feelings to emerge into his consciousness.

It is, after all, primarily the discomfort, the hazardousness of emotion that we wish to be protected from. It is the pain of our own emotions that makes us flee from them.

That is why it is particularly the acceptance of negative emotions that needs to be declared blessed. Those searing and humiliating times when we are too distressed to accommodate ourselves to the requirements of our unsympathetic world, when even the church tends to confront us with its wooden-faced puritanism of 'joy', these are the very times upon which the Lord pronounces his benediction.

Of course this does not simply contradict the Pauline injunction to rejoice always. But it does help to situate it. And, as an initial observation, let us just remark that a capacity for real enjoyment is inseparable from a capacity for real distress. Joy was never truly preserved by a frantic avoidance of wretchedness. The person who is constantly on the defensive against unhappiness is unlikely to be very happy. The naïve hedonism by which some of our contemporaries seem to want to live has not been obviously successful in producing any results except frustration, and our libertarian age, with its frantic quest for pleasure and excitement, is oddly characterized by an increase in the number of people complaining to their doctors that they can no longer feel anything at all.[1]

To an age suffering from affectlessness, 'Blessed are those who mourn' is, paradoxically, a more necessary message than 'Rejoice in the Lord always' because there can be no true rejoicing until we have stopped running away from mourning.

But this is not the only reason why mourning is pronounced blessed. To pursue the meaning of our beatitude further, we must once again return to the consideration of the whole strategy of redemption. Why was it 'necessary' for the Christ to suffer (Luke 24:26)? Why is it that only those who are willing to take up their cross can be accounted his followers (Matt. 10:38 etc)? What sense is there in St Paul's claiming to be 'filling up what is lacking in the sufferings of Christ' (Col. 1:24)?

Surely there is only one answer to these questions: Christ had to suffer and die because suffering and death were where mankind was. If he was to redeem mankind, he had to go, like the good shepherd, to where the lost sheep was. The point is dramatically made in the story of the harrowing of Hell. That is where man was. That is where Christ went to fetch him.[2] Any other kind of redemption would have been a fake, it would not have been a true redemption of true mankind.

But a similar realism is called for on the part of those to be redeemed. We must acknowledge where we are if we are to be redeemed from there.

This is in accordance with man's peculiar position in creation. Man is not just passive, even in his own creation. Man is God's co-worker (cf. 1 Cor. 3:9), he is co-creator even of himself. In St Gregory of Nyssa's startling phrase, each man has to be his own begetter.[3]

Similarly with redemption. It is not, of course, that man has anything of his own to contribute to it independently of God. But, when he is dealing with man, God's act creates a corresponding act in man. God's act does not let man off doing it for himself; it is rather the other way about. 'Work out your own salvation . . . because it is God who works within you' (Phil. 2:12f).

This means that God's acceptance of our pain, in Christ, creates a corresponding acceptance in us of our own pain. It is because Christ has carried the cross of each one of us that we have to carry our own and one anothers' crosses.

Human beings are created interdependent on one another, as we can see even from our biological interconnectedness. We are involved in 'creating' one another. Because of sin, we are also involved in devastating one another. But redemption does not separate us off from one another, however prudent such a move might seem to us; we are involved in redeeming one another. So we are told, 'Carry each other's burdens and in this way you will fulful the law of Christ' (Gal. 6:2).

If we want to know what man really is, in his state of brokenness and fallenness, we must look at Christ in his agony. *Ecce homo* (John 19:5). That is what we are. And it is a double revelation. That is what we are: his agony, his helplessness, his dying, they are all ours. But even worse, that is what we are: we are the people who do that, who kill and torment, who react to love, even to God's love, with that kind of fury, that kind of cruelty, that kind of cynical mockery. *Ecce homo*. In the light of that, is it not right to weep?

In the rather artificial scheme devised by St Augustine for linking

62

the seven beatitudes with the seven gifts of the Holy Spirit, this beatitude of the mourners is linked with the gift of knowledge.[4] To know the truth of our human predicament is to know it as something that can be met only with mourning.

And this is the kernel of true contrition. It is more than likely that St Matthew was thinking especially of penitential mourning in our beatitude,[5] and it is precisely penitential mourning that results from an honest awareness of what man is and that it is, in one way or another, man himself who has made himself what he is.

But yet, blessed are whose who mourn. On the face of it, seeing the human condition clearly for what it is is little more than a formula for despair. The author of 4 Esdras presents himself as replying to a divine communication:

> This is the first thing I want to say and it is the last: it would have been better for the earth never to have brought Adam forth, or, once he had been brought forth, for him to have been constrained not to sin. What use is that we all live now in sadness and have only punishment to hope for when we are dead?[6]

But the Christian does not simply see the human condition in itself. In the broken face of a man he sees the broken yet redeeming face of Christ. And, perhaps even more importantly, he knows that he is not alone in his seeing of the human plight. If we are courageous and humble enough to see it clearly for what it is, that very seeing is a way of identifying ourselves with Christ. Our mourning becomes a singularly profound mode of identification with his redeeming suffering of our lot.

It is vital to realize that, in one sense, this leaves everything exactly as it was before. Uniting our suffering with that of Christ does not, in some mysterious way, change the actual quality of our suffering. It gives it a different perspective, which may make it more possible for us to live with it. But suffering remains suffering, and it hurts.[7] And it hurts body and soul. It weakens our drive and lessens our energy.

People sometimes dream of a heroic acceptance of suffering as if they could bear immense physical pain or immense mental hurt with equanimity. They want to bear their cross jauntily, somehow not minding it. But surely de Caussade and Thérèse of Lisieux are right: the real grace is that we can bear our cross *feebly*.[8] It is part of the cross that we have to bear, that we do not have the energy to bear it.

Our Lord's example is essential here. We must not think of his drawing on infinite resources of Godhead to help him endure his human pain, as if he somehow had a better 'backed' humanity than ours. The incarnation involves no blurring of distinctions, no confusing of the two natures. It was with human resources that he had to bear his human distress, and the New Testament makes it quite clear that his human resources, like ours, were stretched to the limit. 'My soul is disturbed,' as St John makes him say as he goes to his passion (12:27). He knows, as we do, the psychic upset consequent upon pain. 'My God, my God, why have you abandoned me?' he exclaims as he reaches the point of death, according to St Matthew (27:46). He does not see light at the end of the tunnel; he knows what is perhaps the cruellest pain of all, the sense that it is all utterly pointless.

The mourning which our Lord declares to be blessed is no mild discomfort serving chiefly to make life interesting, it is no largely fanciful malaise with which to while away the time. 'In the days of his flesh, he prayed with great shouting and tears' (Hebr. 5:7). That is our Lord's agony. Again, St Thérèse of Lisieux is the notable modern example, facing the blackness of despair and meaninglessness, gazing into the abyss and seeing there only darkness, the darkness of *le néant*.[9]

There is no room here for mock heroics. There is a kind of mourning, a kind of suffering, that we almost deliberately work up to achieve an effect. It is, in certain moods, satisfying to dramatize ourselves to ourselves, if not to others. That is not what our Lord is referring to in this beatitude.

Or we can exploit our real or imagined upsets to give ourselves an excuse for evading more real discomforts and responsibilities in life, or to secure attention to ourselves, or sympathy, or even to give ourselves an identity in this faceless world of ours. But all of these are spurious reactions. Maybe they are symptomatic of a genuine disorder, in that it is a disorder not to be able to face life without resorting to such kinds of deception. But in that case, it is the genuine disorder, not the 'emotional' decoration, that is of significance for our Christian lives. And the truth is usually less dramatic than we should like it to be.

The suffering that our Lord pronounces blessed is the genuine suffering of an honest awareness of and involvement in the breakdown of our world, our society, ourselves. It is the mourning of the realist, the penitent. Different people are inserted into it in different ways, but it comes to all of us, because all of us, in this world, are heading for death. However splendidly the 'inner man' is being renewed day by day by the Holy Spirit, the outer man—and that includes our psyche as well as our bodies—is still decaying day by day and will eventually die (2 Cor. 4:16). It is our own involvement in death that is redeemed by Christ's death, [10] and it is this which is pronounced to be blessed.

There is no room for antics in face of death. It is the real pain of it that constitutes our way into the passion of Christ. And it is part of that pain that we should wish to be rid of it. And this means that it is part of that pain that we should resort to painkillers of one kind or another. We must be humble enough to do this. We must receive God's gift of the 'wine that makes man's heart happy' (Ps. 104:15). It is a merciful provision in God's world that we are not required to be totally conscious the whole time. Apart from chemical narcotics like wine, there is the precious gift of sleep, of companionship, of books, of sheer numbness. We must not be ashamed to admit that we need relief sometimes in ways like these.

But we must not become so addicted to narcotics that we come to forget what and where we are. Narcotics must be part of our realism, not an escape from it.

And one narcotic that is perhaps particularly damaging is the narcotic of 'doing something about it'. Of course there is often something to be done about all kinds of things, and it is natural enough to try to do it. But we must not deceive ourselves. However much we do about however many things, we are still, ultimately, faced with the helplessness of the human condition. No amount of achievement can overcome death. The final remedy for the human condition is totally in the hands of God, and it is beyond death. All else is only shifting the heavy suitcase from one hand to the other.

It is important, then, that we give due value to the situations which have us stumped. There is a not unnatural tendency among us to concentrate our attention on those problems which we think we can solve, and then to try to pretend that these are the only problems. But the ultimate problems are problems that we cannot solve. We cannot solve the problems of sin or death. Only God can solve these.

This is why it is so important to mourn. Mourning is the recognition of our true plight. Beyond all that we can tackle, there is the total problem of what we are. And that is beyond us. And it confronts us with the sorry truth of fallen man. And unless we are totally insensitive, what other response is there but to mourn?

This impinges on different people in different ways; but it is important to be quite clear that it impinges on us essentially in our own pain, whether that pain be brought about by physical causes or emotional causes or whatever. It has sometimes been suggested that we ought to make a sharp distinction between the pain that we undergo as a consequence of our own fallenness, and the pain that we undergo redemptively in union with the suffering of Christ for the sake of others. On the basis of this distinction, it has further been suggested that, if we have faith, we ought normally to be freed even in this life from all our own pain. Then, if God so wills it, we shall be given a different pain for the good of others. But this is arrant nonsense. There is only one pain, and that is the pain caused by sin, original sin, accumulated sin and personal sin. It is that pain that Christ carried on the cross, and it is that pain that we must carry with him, and our normal part in it is precisely the pain that arises from our own fallenness. Even if we are given the privilege of carrying other people's burdens too, these will normally be related to the burden which arises from our own psychosomatic condition. The cross that we must carry is the cross of ourselves. There is no justification whatsoever for fanciful dichotomies, and no reason whatsoever to believe that we ought, in this life, to be freed from our own personal pains. We may indeed be freed from some of them, but the final remedy is given only at the end, at the resurrection from the dead. Until then we are in mortal bodies, which cannot help but diminish the vitality of our mental and emotional processes. It is only at the resurrection that we shall have bodies which are capable of total well-being.

This means that we have no right to be arrogant or cavalier in our way of confronting pain, our own or anyone else's. Of course it is all caused by sin—the very word 'pain' indicates its link with penance—but it must still be respected. There is a striking scene in Charles Williams' Arthuriad, when Galahad at last arrives at the Castle of the Grail, Carbonek; instead of going straight in triumphantly, he kneels down in the archway:

> The astonished angels of the spirit heard him moan:
>   *Pardon, lord; pardon and bless me, father.*
>
> Doubtfully stood the celestial myrmidons, scions
> of unremitted beauty; bright feet paused.
> Aching with the fibrous infelicity of time,
>   pierced his implacability, Galahad kneeled.
>   . . . .
>
> Under the arch the Merciful Child
> wept for the grief of his father in reconciliation.
>   . . . .
>
> 'Forgive Us', the High Prince said, 'for Our existence;
> forgive the means of grace and the hope of glory.'[11]

C. S. Lewis' comment on this episode is very much to the point:

> Christians naturally think more often of what the world has inflicted on the saints; but the saints also inflict much on the world. Mixed with the cry of martyrs, the cry of nature wounded by Grace also ascends—and presumably to heaven. . . . (Williams) had no belief in a conception of Grace which simply abolishes nature; and he felt that there was always something legitimate in the protests of nature against the harrowing operation of conversion.[12]

Indeed, every work of blessing is also a work of destruction, and what has to be destroyed is never pure wrongness, however riddled with wrongness it may be. There is no such thing as pure wrongness. Even the most appalling wickedness is only goodness gone wrong, and its pain is therefore still a noble pain. And the pain of its doom is still a noble pain.

Christian mourning is a mourning of great delicacy, which does not despise or criticize or condemn.

Indeed, if there is anything which distinguishes redemptive pain from any other, it is to be found here. Redemptive pain is ordinary

67

pain known to be united with Christ. That is to say, it is pain that has become compassion, suffering *with*. It is our own suffering, but it is known to be a suffering taken on by Christ, and so united with all other suffering. It is personal to us, but even as such it is, almost, impersonal, universal. Passion becomes compassion through the passion of Christ.

And this is where it becomes plain how the beatitude of those who mourn is concerned with charity. Merely being miserable usually makes us selfish. But being miserable in Christ opens it out again. And it is this that takes it beyond the petulance of 'this should not be happening to me', to a more basic, therefore more inconsolable, woe, which forgoes the luxury of indignation, and enters into the mystery of divine love, scooping up fallen man in his totality from the depths of his ruin, and gently tending him towards perfection. In the depth of Hell, hope reawakens. And this is the utterly pure grief: it knows that there is nothing more to do; but it also knows that 'whatever the Lord wants, he does' (Ps. 135:6).

It is at this depth that our beatitude becomes one with the precept to rejoice always in the Lord. That rejoicing is the purity of a grief that has become deeper than whining self-pity, that has come to rest in the infinitely blissful sacrificial love of God himself.

And a major part of its bliss is its hope. Not its optimism, for it has none, but its hope; its conviction that God's love is able to bring life even out of death. Blessed are those who mourn, for they will be comforted. There is a kind of mourning which seeks no comfort, because it has settled down. 'A prison gets to be a friend,' as the American poetess, Emily Dickinson, wrote.[13] There is even a kind of mourning which would refuse comfort, because it prefers the certainty of permanency: we can identify ourselves with our grief, so that we could accept consolation only at the expense of losing ourselves. In the words of Heine:

> I am unhappy Atlas! A whole world,
> A universe of griefs I have to bear;
> Unbearable I bear it, and my heart
> Within me longs to break.

Proud heart of mine! You longed for this, yes, this:
You wanted to be blessed, for ever blessed,
Or else for ever wretched, my proud heart:
And wretched now you are.[14]

In some ways the hardest thing of all is to go on grieving honestly, and not to distort our very grief into a spurious contentment.

But the mourning which is pronounced blessed by Christ is a mourning which yearns for relief, but is not prepared to be fobbed off with anything less than relief. It has seen mankind in its fallenness, and nothing less will satisfy it than mankind fully restored. And so it has its joy in the Lord, in whom already mankind is made whole; but it mourns deeply and cannot but mourn until all things are made new in Christ.

Chapter Eight

Blessed are those who hunger and thirst for righteousness, for they will have their fill.

Once again we find ourselves faced with a beatitude which exists in two versions, one of which seems to be a more spiritualized version of the other. The Lucan version, which is presumably the more basic, says simply, 'Blessed are you who hunger now, for you will have your fill' (Luke 6:21). There is also a corresponding woe, 'Woe to you who are full now, for you will be hungry' (Luke 6:25).

The immediate sense of this is so embarrassingly obvious that it excludes even the possibility of commentary. It is part of the radical upturning of everything announced by our Lord, and summed up in the devastating principle that 'the last shall be first and the first last' (Matt. 20:16).

A principle of such utterly stark simplicity cannot helpfully be taken as indicating a programme of action; there is nothing you can *do* about it. To stop eating or to curtail it to a minimum would not of itself achieve much, and it would run headlong into other items of New Testament teaching, such as St Paul's equally simple and liberating doctrine of food (Rom. 14). It would also run into the nickname earned by our Lord himself, 'glutton and boozer' (Matt. 11:19).

These aphoristic declarations which fall so readily from the lips of Christ are surely meant to startle us into new ways of thinking, new ways of evaluating, and so, in this indirect way, sometimes into new ways of behaving too.

And it was almost bound to happen that one fruit of such new thinking would be more digested versions of the same beatitude.

And we find one such in St Matthew, 'Blessed are those who hunger and thirst for righteousness, for they will have their fill.'

But it is worth halting the moralizing process for a moment a little bit sooner than this. It is worth considering the significance of hungering in more obvious ways, before we turn to the specific hunger indicated by St Matthew, the hunger for righteousness.

As we saw in our consideration of the previous beatitude, redemption does not involve the suppression of our emotions, but rather their rectifying. Similarly it does not involve the suppression, but rather the rectifying, of our appetites.

It is indeed important that we should know how to say 'No' to our appetites, but that is not because appetites, as such, are bad, but because our appetites are often astray. And it is not really the fault of our appetites that they are astray; it is, to use a convenient American word, far more the fault of our whole 'mindset'. Without wishing to follow the Stoics the whole way in regarding all disorders in human life as being fundamentally mistakes in reason, it is surely the case that the basic disorder is often a disorder of reason. Our unhelpful reactions are a product of an unhelpful way of seeing things.

Consider two of the commonest ways in which our appetites go wrong. First of all, we are all of us liable to be bamboozled by advertising. And this does not only refer to overt advertising; there is a great deal of advertising implicit simply in cultural values and assumptions, and therefore in education, for example, and popular journalism, not to mention political utterances. As a result of this kind of pressure, we come to believe that it is desirable to have the latest colour TV set, three or four motor-cars, a university education, uncensored entertainment, and so on, in complete abstraction from all the particular circumstances that make people so different from one another. We forget to ask ourselves whether we really do want such things. Society or the advertisers decide that question for us in advance. We find ourselves, unless we are careful, caught up in pre-packed needs and desires, which may actually have very little to do with our genuine appetites.

And secondly, we are sometimes guilty of abstracting general principles from our appetites. C. S. Lewis, in one of the works which comprise his space trilogy, describes very perceptively how his hero becomes conscious of this temptation on the planet Venus:

71

As he let the empty gourd fall from his hand and was about to pluck a second one, it came into his head that he was now neither hungry nor thirsty. And yet to repeat a pleasure so intense and almost so spiritual seemed an obvious thing to do. His reason, or what we commonly take to be reason in our own world, was all in favour of tasting this miracle again. . . . Yet something seemed opposed to this 'reason'. It is difficult to suppose that this opposition came from desire, for what desire would turn from so much deliciousness? But for whatever cause, it appeared to him better not to taste again. . . . He stood pondering over this and wondering how often in his life on Earth he had reiterated pleasures not through desire, but in the teeth of desire and in obedience to a spurious rationalism.[1]

Another way of abstracting from our appetites is to hoard. Our Lord tells us to pray for our daily bread, and that is realistic. But most of us prefer to have a few days' extra supply in hand, and that can become dangerous. It is not necessarily wicked to keep something in reserve, and it may be a very reasonable way of saving time and energy for other things; by the middle of the thirteenth century, for example, the Dominicans had abandoned their original principle of not keeping any food in the house for more than one day at a time, because they found that going out every day to beg for the day's food was making it impossible for them to get on with their study and their preaching.[2] That is a realistic assessment of a situation. But it can get out of hand. It is interesting to see how Evagrius defines gluttony:

The thought of gluttony very quickly makes a monk abandon his ascetic discipline. It sketches before his mind his stomach, his liver, his spleen, long sickness, running out of food, no doctor. . . . It reminds him often of particular brothers to whom this kind of thing has happened. Sometimes it even prompts such brothers to go and visit those who are practising abstinence and tell them about their misfortunes and how they were all due to their asceticism.[3]

We notice that it is not really anything to do with hunger. It is the mind, daydreaming, that demands the extra food, not the stomach. And surely the mind is, in the last analysis, the wrong organ to employ in this concern. Hunger must be restored to the stomach, it does not belong to the imagination.

St Gregory of Nyssa very blandly dismisses the literal interpretation of the rules given in Exodus for eating the passover. The law, he says, does not have to tell us how to eat, because 'nature is a sufficient lawgiver in such matters, placing in us our appetite for food'.[4] That is all that needs to be said about it. It is the belly that is the measure of the appropriate quantity of food.[5]

Evagrius' remedy for gluttony is that we should make ourselves hungry,[6] and surely this is a sensible way of trying to face up to both kinds of disorder that we have been considering. Hunger confronts us with a genuine appetite, which will then show up the hollowness of many of our supposed 'desires'.

There is a revealing little story in the Sayings of the Desert Fathers about a monk who was feeling restless in the desert and could not make up his mind whether to stay there or not. So he went to abba Paphnutius to get advice. The old man told him, 'Sit in your cell. Say just one prayer in the morning and one in the evening and one at night; and when you are hungry, eat, and when you are thirsty, drink, and when you are sleepy, go to bed. And remain in the desert.' The young man was not convinced, so he went along to consult abba John. Abba John made only one comment: 'Do not say any prayer at all, just sit in your cell.' The young man was still not satisfied, so he went on to abba Arsenius, and explained the whole situation to him. Arsenius simply said, 'Keep to what the fathers have told you; I have nothing more to say to you than what they have already said.' At last the young man was convinced.[7]

The point of this advice is that the very foundation of the spiritual life must be a basic realism about what it means to be human; and one way to bring ourselves face to face with our own essential humanity is to confine ourselves to our essential appetites. And they must not be decorated even with piety. The young monk must learn to respond to his basic needs of hunger, thirst, tiredness, and only then will there be a basis of human truth on which to build a life of prayer. If he by-passes this, his spiritual life will be nothing more than fantasy.

And, of course, one of the results of such a return to fundamentals is that a man will discover that he is a dependent being. The trouble with being too well off (in whatever way) is that it can help us to deceive ourselves into thinking that we are, more or less, indepen-

dent. And the quest for independence is one of fallen man's most
besetting blunders. Man is not meant to be independent. He is
dependent in all kinds of ways on all kinds of things. If his religion
is to be real, it must start from a profound acknowledgement of this
fact. Man is dependent on God, of course; but he is also dependent
on a wide range of creatures. This is how God has made him. He
can, certainly, make himself artificially dependent on some things
which are not strictly necessary; but it is a far more disastrous
mistake to try to make himself independent of things on which he
is meant to be dependent.

A basic rhythm in man's life is that of need or desire, and the
satisfaction of that need or desire. Man's redemption involves the
recovery of that pattern.

And a consequence of such a recovery is likely to be a greatly
enhanced sense of appreciation. As has been said often enough,
there is no sauce so effective and so cheap as hunger.[8] The further
we live from our basic appetites, the more jaded our palates become,
the more blasé our attitudes to things, and the more unresponsive
in general we become.

But the programme of returning to our basic appetites should not
be interpreted in a puritanical way. God's world is an extravagant
one, and our appetites are accordingly diverse and exuberant. The
recognition of real needs should lead us to a recognition of real
luxuries. So long as we confuse the two, we shall not appreciate
either properly. The more clearly we grasp what it means to pray,
precisely, for our daily bread ('bread of our need', as the Syriac
version has it), the more we shall be able to enjoy all the rest as
uncovenanted extras.

After all, the beatitude does not promise to the hungry that they
will be given a bare sufficiency, but that they 'will be filled', 'stuffed
full'. If they are filled, that means that they have everything that
they could possibly want. As St Thomas teaches, no authentic desire
is created in vain.[9] Beatitude means 'having everything you want',
according to St Augustine's definition, qualified only by the rider,
'and wanting nothing wrongly'.[10]

But unfortunately the more aware and appreciative we become
in this world, the more we cannot help but notice that many of our
desires are in fact constantly being thwarted. We discover that there
is a painful misfit between ourselves and our world.

This at once raises the question whether we ought not therefore to go out and oblige the world to conform to our desires. But this avenue is blocked by the beatitude of the meek, the helpless. The misfit between our desires and our world is in part at least a result of a misfit between our authentic, God-given, nature and our actual desires. It would be a disaster to let us simply remodel the world in accordance with what we consciously want. We should succeed only in building a tower of Babel, overcoming the mercy that sought to defeat our vain ambition.

But if we are not to rebuild the world in accordance with our specifications, are we instead to try to conform ourselves resignedly to the world as it is? If we cannot have what we want, should we try to want what we have, as the Stoics would have us do?[11] That avenue is blocked off by the beatitude of the mourners and our own present one. We are to keep our appetites, in spite of their apparent impossibility of fulfilment.

And this brings us to St Matthew's version of the beatitude. 'Blessed are those who hunger and thirst for righteousness.' Surely the righteousness in question here can be connected with the righteousness of God's kingdom, which our Lord says should be the primary object of our seeking (Matt. 6:33). And this must mean, ultimately, the total right order which goes with God's establishment of his kingdom, including the right ordering of our lives, which is what our personal righteousness consists of. And it is perhaps pertinent to recall that God's law comes fully into effect only in the Promised Land (Deut. 4:14); as Barnabas reminds us, justification, the making righteous of man, is an eschatological hope rather than a present reality.[12] There is an eschatological slant to any whole-hearted yearning for righteousness.

The misfit between our appetites and our world serves to give us a chance to purify and disentangle our desires, to bring them in line with God's total rightness, so that we can discover that the most basic appetite of all is precisely the appetite for God and for his order.

The instinct to remake the world is true to this extent, that the world must be remade for our full contentment; but it must be remade by God in accordance with his specifications, not by us in accordance with ours. And so the Stoics are right to this extent, that our desires must be conformed, not to the existing state of affairs, but to the God-given truth of the whole created order. But that, of course, includes the God-given truth of our own appetites.

And it is because we hope in God's promise of a new heaven and a new earth, and a new heart for ourselves, that we cannot simply deny our appetites. There is meant to be a harmony between our wants and our world, but that harmony is the orchestration of one basic theme, which is the intended union of God and man in love.

It is the desire for God which is the most fundamental appetite of all, and it is an appetite we can never eliminate. We may seek to disown it, but it will not go away. If we deny that it is there, we shall in fact only divert it to some other object or range of objects. And that will mean that we invest some creature or creatures with the full burden of our need for God, a burden which no creature can carry. No colour television, no human love, no religious life, no activity, can finally assuage our hunger for God. If, like the prodigal son, we 'return to ourselves', like him we shall recognize that we have been trying to fill our bellies with husks, and we shall turn our minds towards home, towards our Father's love.

In a magnificent stroke of genius, Chaucer adapts the sad story of Troilus and Cressida to make this point. Where Boccaccio simply leaves Troilus dead on the battlefield and concludes with cynical advice to young men to set their hearts on mature women rather than on flighty lasses,[13] Chaucer takes us up to heaven with the 'buoyant soul' of Troilus to the intellectual vision and audition of the stars.[14] Cressida's infidelity is presented, at least in retrospect, not so much as a personal sin, though it is that, but rather as a typical instance of the instability of everything in this world:

> Such is this world. If you can see it right,
> You'll find but little heart's rest anywhere.
> God grant that we may take it for the best![15]

As Troilus looks down from heaven, he sees 'this little spot of earth' and realizes that it is really not worth bothering about; by comparison with 'the full felicity that is in heaven above', it is nothing. Finally he looks down at the place where he had been killed

> And in himself he laughed to see the woe
> Of those who mourned so sadly at his death.[16]

Chaucer concludes with an appeal to young people which is very different in tone from Boccaccio's peroration:

O young fresh folks, both he and she,
In whom love burgeons with your time of life,
Repair you home from worldly vanity,
And of your heart cast up the eager face
To God who in his image fashioned you,
And think this world is nothing but a fair,
This world which passes quick as flowers fair.

And give your love to him who, out of love,
Upon a cross, our souls for to redeem,
First died, then rose and sits in heaven above;
For he will surely not deceive the man
Who will his heart all wholly set on him.
And since he is the best for us to love
And the least proud, why seek pretended loves?[17]

Our natural need to love 'returns home' when it turns to God; he is the truly faithful lover, who will never let us down. All the fascinating delights of this world on which we set our hearts so easily are really not substantial or constant enough to give us 'full felicity'. This need not necessarily mean that we should simply spurn them; but they will only make satisfying sense if they are kept firmly in the context of our most basic need, our most basic aspiration, which is that for God and for the fullness of heavenly bliss.

It is around this central need that all our other needs and desires fall into place. Without it, they cannot help but be disordered, and no attempt to reduce them to order will have much effect except further disorder.

In the *Cloud of Unknowing* we find a question raised that was evidently vexing some spiritual people: how should they regulate their external behaviour in such matters as food and conversation? The *Cloud* refuses to answer these questions directly. Instead it moves on to the crucial question: how much should you practise love of God in the contemplative darkness which the book recommends? And here the answer comes ringing out: you should love God without any restraint or moderation at all. And then everything else will simply fall into place, so the only advice given about how

77

much sleep we should take, how much food, how much drink, and so on, is that we should be 'reckless': 'Take what you can get!'[18]

Our appetites need to be controlled because they are out of tune, out of harmony with our need for God. But control is only a temporary measure. The ideal is for us not to control our appetites at all, but to allow them full rein in the wake of an uncontrolled appetite for God.

It is important to take seriously the implication of our beatitude that there really is an appetite for God, and for his righteousness. We all too easily speak and think as if righteousness resulted chiefly from the curbing of our appetites, as if our appetites were only for sin. But strictly speaking we have no appetite for sin. What we experience as an appetite for sin is a sick appetite which has mistaken its object. In moments of despondency we may perhaps look around and think that we should be much happier if we gave up trying to be good, if we could enjoy all the vices of the world around us. But that is only a fantasy. The desire for goodness is really a much more robust desire than any alleged desire for evil. And it is the *desire* for goodness which we must cherish. Sometimes we can be too much preoccupied with seeming good, even with being good in the sense of conforming our outward behaviour to external standards of correctness, and as a result ignore our own real needs. We must be content to grow slowly towards goodness, taking, if need be, a long time to convalesce. Most of us, maybe, will still be barely at the beginning of our recovery even when we die. But that is better than killing ourselves pretending to be healthy.

The appetite for God and all the concomitant appetites that form its ordered escort make a desire too vast for most of us really to face up to all at once. Part, at least, of the disorder of our desires arises from a certain timidity, which prefers even small delights which are near at hand and easily obtained to larger delights which are more uncertain and difficult to acquire. We have trivialized ourselves, fobbing ourselves off with trinkets when we wanted a kingdom.

Blessed are those who have at least begun to hunger and thirst for righteousness, who refuse to be fobbed off. But woe also to them, in this world, for they will be perpetually dissatisfied, perpetually crying out for more. 'Thy kingdom come' is their earnest prayer. 'O Lord, how much longer?' (Ps. 6:4 etc.).

78

But the waiting is not entirely without its purpose or without its consolations.

Those great Romantic psychologists of Christian spirituality, the Cistercian Fathers, tell us that the bridegroom keeps the bride waiting so long to sharpen and increase her desire.[19] And, as St Thomas says, desire is the faculty which receives, so that the bigger our desire is, the more we can receive.[20] The promise is that those who hunger and thirst will be 'stuffed full', and no meagre appetite will suffice for the immensity of blessing which God intends for his faithful lovers. Our part in this life is to learn to want largely and earnestly enough to make us capable of the infinite rightness of God's kingdom. It is no good coming with a thimble and saying that all we want is a little drop of water. God has nothing less to give than everything. It really is a case of all or nothing. And it is in vain to plead that it is too big for us. Of course it is too big for us. But we are all the same made for that which is too big for us. We ourselves are too big for us. The more we try to tame and reduce ourselves and our desires and hopes, the more we deceive and distort ourselves. We are made for God and nothing less will really satisfy us.

So we must allow our innate appetite for infinity to dislodge us whenever we are inclined to settle down and call it a day.

And the consolations that do come to us must be allowed to whet our appetites, for that is what they are for. Guigo II, the Carthusian, explaining why our life in this world consists of such erratic alternations of consolation and desolation, of contemplative closeness to Christ and a sense that we have been abandoned by him, says that if we were given too much consolation in this life, and given it too continuously, we might forget that God has more for us and confuse the journey with our home-coming.[21]

It is interesting that St Basil treats both the supernatural gifts we now enjoy in the church and the natural gifts in the world around us as different kinds of foretaste of paradise.[22] They must be appreciated as such, and appreciated as lavishly as they are given; but they are meant to give us a taste for more, not to make our appetites dull and lethargic.

The essential point is made clearly in Meister Eckhart's *Talks of Instruction*:

God gives no gift, God never has given any gift, in order that anyone should have the gift and rest content with it. Rather, all the gifts that he has ever given, in heaven and on earth, were given in view of his single purpose, to give *one* gift, which is himself. With all these other gifts he wants to prepare us now for the gift which is himself; and all the works he has brought about in heaven and on earth were done simply to enable him to perform one work, namely to make himself blessed in making us blessed. This is why I say, in all gifts and works we must learn to see God, and not let ourselves be content with anything, not allow ourselves to settle down with anything. In this life there is no settling down for us in any way, and there never was for any man, however far he may have progressed.[23]

It is truly our whole set of appetites that must be involved in our Christian growth. We shall not succeed in loving God the more, just because we succeed in loving creatures less. As St Thomas says, it is no way to give glory to the Creator to despise his creation.[24] We must allow a healthy wanting to be formed in us through all our diverse experience of life, with the Holy Spirit working inwardly to turn it all into 'ordered love' (cf. Cant. 2:4 Vulgate).

Though we may, from time to time, have to brake firmly to stop ourselves rushing headlong into silly satisfactions that will only militate against the final, total satisfaction of beatitude, we must not make braking a whole way of life. It is more important, eventually, to know how to say 'Yes' to a desire than to know how to say 'No'. At the end we shall have to surrender ourselves utterly and recklessly and without any inhibition to the overwhelming attractiveness of God, and in so doing also to surrender ourselves with all that we are to the glorified perfection of all that he has made.

The forsaking—or sometimes the impossibility—of immediate gratification should not make us suspicious or cynical or despairing of gratification as such. It is our surprising lot in this world to have to live with our desires and keep them alive and cherish them, so that at the end we can be content to be 'stuffed full'. Parsimony is not necessarily a good education for heaven.

And it is surely not too hard to see how all of this is really related to charity. It is, as the pseudo-Dionysius reminds us, characteristic of love to be 'ecstatic', in the sense that it puts the lover 'outside himself ',[25] it makes him belong to the other, which he loves.

80

And that is the risk which fallen man dreads so much. His 'self-possession' is his favoured defence. To want something, whatever it may be, is to put himself at risk.

But no creature can content itself. Our only hope of genuine fulfilment is for us to take that risk and recognize that our joy is outside ourselves. And that is to hunger. Charity situates our good outside ourselves, and knows that that good can never be obtained by any means except its own gift of itself.

The emptiness established by poverty and meekness is an emptiness that paves the way for us to learn how to be dependent for our fullness on another, on God. and it is when that emptiness learns how to yearn, how to hunger and thirst, that it begins to move towards that blessedness which is pronounced upon it. But it. must also learn how to wait, to wait upon the gift that it desires. To grab is to destroy, not because the object of desire is destroyed, but because enjoyment is destroyed. We see this in human affection, and we must know that it is true of God too. To try to secure God for ourselves is to secure only an illusion. And because we have, in sin, set ourselves on the way of security, we must painfully be weaned from it again.

Blessed are those who let themselves hunger and thirst, accepting no substitute for what they truly want, letting all that they are given serve only to whet their appetites for more. They truly are the ones to whom God will give himself in all his fullness.

But that fullness is not for this life. The gift which God makes of himself in this life is known chiefly in the increase of our desire for him.[26] And that desire, being love, is infinite, and so stretches our mortal life to its limits. And that stretching is our most earnest joy, but it is also our most earnest suffering in this life. So those who hunger and thirst are, even now, truly blessed; but their blessedness is that of those who mourn.

Chapter Nine

Blessed are the merciful,
for they will receive mercy.

At this point in the beatitudes, there seems to be a kind of shift into a slightly different key. The beatitude of the merciful, and the two which follow it, are more directly concerned with moral, spiritual values, and are less starkly at odds with the instinctive values of men in the world. But they are very necessary to fill out the picture, to indicate the symptoms of burgeoning charity and to warn us against possible mistakes.

And there is a very serious mistake lurking only just round the corner, if we have followed the course of the beatitudes so far. If we have come to see something of God's righteousness, of his right order for the world, and have begun to feel a hunger for it to be fulfilled, if we have accordingly begun to mourn over the wretched state to which man has reduced himself and his world, then it is more than likely that we shall begin to feel indignant and angry. Anger is, as Evagrius observed, the besetting temptation of those who have begun to see things clearly.[1] It is intolerable that God's world should be so savaged by the folly and the wickedness of men. The more passionately we yearn for the complete justice and integrity of God's kingdom, the more naturally we shall turn with anger towards all that seems to militate against them. 'I was overwhelmed with blazing anger because of the wicked' (Ps. 119:53).

It is to this very natural reaction that our beatitude is addressed. Blessed are the merciful. Our zeal for righteousness must not be allowed to make us hard and ungenerous.

People sometimes talk as if there were a special kind of indignation called 'righteous indignation'. But surely the truth of the matter is that, in one sense, all indignation is 'righteous', but equally all indignation is more than likely, in us, to be contaminated with unrighteousness. 'The anger of man does not achieve the righteousness of God,' according to St James (1:20). Anger, indignation, arise from a genuine intuition of righteousness, but the 'anger of man' mistakes the tactic which is appropriate in face of unrighteousness, and so can never achieve the righteousness of God; at best it can achieve only a kind of symbolic righteousness of men.

But it is nevertheless worth noticing that it is from a genuine insight that all indignation comes. Anger is, in general, such a powerful and alarming phenomenon that we prefer to steer clear of it, in ourselves and in others. But this means that we are generally only very poorly equipped to deal with it when it does arise, and that we are too prone to avoid the situations in which it is likely to arise.

And the major situation in which it is likely to arise is one in which what we know to be the case contrasts sadly with what we know ought to be the case. A flight from anger will almost inevitably mean a flight from vision.

But the beatitudes encourage honesty of vision. It is the man who sees clearly who becomes a mourner, who learns to hunger and thirst for righteousness. And the more clearly he sees, and the more earnestly he hungers, the more reason he will see to be angry. And the more hesitant he will become about dismissing his anger as irrelevant or impertinent.

After all, the righteousness of God for which he hungers is a total rightness, in which everything is made good. Measured against this criterion, even the slightest imperfection is intolerable. The man who yearns for this kind of righteousness can never be fobbed off with the soothing maxim that we 'must make the best of a bad job'. God did not intend us to have to make the best of a bad job; he intended us to make the best of an excellent job.

So even when our anger seems most private and selfish, even when it is caused by purely individual and possibly rather absurd disappointments, it is still, in its own way, the anger of righteousness. Man was not made for disappointments, he was made to have all his real desires fulfilled. Any sense of frustration, however it is brought about, is quite legitimately taken as evidence that something is wrong with the world. Even if we are disappointed because we could not get something we never had any business to want, it is still evidence that there is something wrong with the world.

But this last possibility alerts us to something important. What is wrong with the world includes what is wrong with us. And maybe what is wrong with the world is never entirely unrelated to what is wrong with us.

It would, of course, be absurd to maintain in any superficial sense that we are personally responsible for all the ills that confront us.[2] The doctrine that what we suffer is always proportionate to our own sins and blunders is refuted at length in the book of Job and dismissed without further ado by our Lord himself. The blindness of the man born blind is declared not to be the result of any personal fault of his own or of his parents, any more than the sad fate of those upon whom the tower of Siloam fell was due to their own personal wickedness (John 9:1–3; Luke 13:1–5).

But in a deeper, more elusive, way, the doctrine of Adam shows that none of us can simply distance himself from the ills of the world. We are all Adam,[3] and it is through the sin of Adam that death, with all its train of horrors, entered into the world.

What vitiates the anger of man is its tendency to assume that what is wrong is always 'out there'. But if we let our indignation direct our response only to the evident wrongness 'out there' in the world, we shall end up simply imposing a new pattern of wrongness on things, reflecting the wrongness that there is in ourselves. The 'meek' are pronounced blessed, in part, because they are the ones who forgo the attempt to change things, knowing that any change will merely be a change from one kind of wrongness and incompleteness to another. The anger that goads us into action, if it is just the anger of man, will goad us into action that can never produce perfection. The blessed hunger for righteousness can never be satisfied that way.

Blessed are the merciful, our beatitude says, for they will receive mercy. And this must mean that it is a part of our bliss to receive mercy. And this reminds us that our hunger for righteousness can be satisfied, and our mourning consoled, only if we ourselves receive mercy. And so our attention is drawn to our own share in the wrongness of things. Our own attainment of perfect righteousness must be by way of mercy.

St James warns us that 'there is judgement without mercy for anyone who does not show mercy,' which echoes precisely the terms of our beatitude. But he puts it in a context which can help us to see why it must be so. 'Speak and act as those who are going to be judged by the law of freedom; for there is judgement without mercy for anyone who does not show mercy' (2:12f). At first sight this is a strange conjunction. What has judgement with or without mercy to do with judgement by the law of freedom? And what is the law of freedom anyhow?

In an earlier chapter too, St James mentions the law of freedom, and it is interesting to see how many of the themes that we find in the beatitudes are gathered together in this passage.

> Let everyone be quick to hear, slow to speak, slow to anger; for the anger of man does not achieve the righteousness of God. So put off all filth and abundance of malice, and receive in meekness the implanted word which can save your souls. And be doers of the word, not just hearers who deceive themselves. Anyone who is a hearer of the word and not a doer is like a man who notices his natural face in a mirror and then, having noticed himself, goes away and immediately forgets what kind of man he is. But the man who peeps into the perfect law, the law of freedom, and then remains there, being not just a hearer who forgets but a doer in fact, blessed shall he be in his doing (1:19–25).

St James is, perhaps, not the clearest and most logical of writers. But he is evidently making certain connexions. The law of freedom is in some way like a mirror, in which a man can see what he looks like. But it is also identical with, or at least intimately related to, the 'implanted word which can save your souls'. And this implanted word is surely the word of God by which he created us. At the very core of our being is what God says we are, and that, of course, is what we are, for God 'spoke and it happened' (Ps. 33:9). It is the fundamental truth of our nature, our identity, our very existence. And of course it must also be the 'law of our freedom', because it is always and only the truth that sets us free (John 8:32). So long as we are constrained, by whatever factors, into being something other than what we are, we are unfree. But what we are is what God says we are. So long, then, as we are other than what God says we are, we are a lie and in bondage. And there is nothing that can save us except that original truth of God's creative word.

And surely it is precisely in this word which lurks at the core of our existence, that we must learn to see what we are, as in a mirror. But seeing what we are in God will also and inevitably show up what we are, existentially, in ourselves. And that is, for most of us, a disturbing eventuality. This is why most of us just peep and run. But if we can peep and stay there, then the truth of what we are will become effective in us, we shall become doers as well as hearers, and we shall be blessed in our doing.

Now this surely shows us what it means to be judged by the law of freedom, and why the prospect of that judgement can be linked with the threat of judgement without mercy if we do not show mercy. The law of freedom is the very law of our being. We are judged, not by some extrinsic measure, but simply by the truth of what we are in God's making.[4] And by that standard, we must confess that we have all fallen short of the glory for which we were made (Rom. 3:23).

So long as we are content to judge by external standards, we can probably find ways of reassuring ourselves that we are not doing too badly; we can compare ourselves with others and find that at least we are better than some. And inevitably we shall choose standards of judgement which enable us to do this. Once we cut loose from the essential standard of God's creative word, we shall immediately begin to look for criteria which seem to us to justify ourselves. Self-justification is one of fallen man's favourite occupations. And it will nearly always be found to involve justification of oneself by condemnation of others.

But the law of freedom, the truth of what we are by God's creating, is a far less malleable standard, which cannot be reshaped to our own superficial advantage. The truth can set us free, but only on its own terms. But if its terms are accepted, then indeed that law of freedom, that implanted word, can save our souls. Whatever we may have become through sin, God's word abides for ever. There is in him, not in us, the constant possibility of our remaking, because he does not retract his word. To gaze into the truth of our creation is at once to see the extent of our shortcomings and to see the possibility of our complete perfecting. To judge by this standard is, therefore, always to judge with mercy; it is to recognize exactly what has to be condemned, but in that very recognition to see also the possibility of new hope. And, so long as this life shall last, nobody can be excluded from that possibility.

86

The word which can save us is not our word, it does not depend on any residual capacity for good which we can claim as our own; it is God's word, and its inexhaustible power to bring life out of death, perfection out of disaster, is simply its power to create being out of non-being. There are no more qualifications presupposed on our side than there are for our creation.

It is in this way, then, that we must learn to see clearly the sorry world of our sinfulness. We must see it without illusion, and we must yearn for a better world; but all of this must come from a persevering attentiveness to the creative word of God, which, in disallowing complacency and self-justification, at the same time disallows despair of anyone.

It also disallows selectiveness. The righteousness for which we must hunger and thirst is a total righteousness. The 'implanted word' in which we glimpse that righteousness and conceive an appetite for it, is not just a law of our own individual existence, nor is it simply the law of the individual existence of others; it is the law of all creation. In God's one word all things were made, and the word implanted in us, though unique in the sense that it brings us to a unique existence, is nevertheless also universal, because God has only one Word.[5] All the multiplicity, the rich diversity, that there is in creation is but the manifold expression of the 'one thing' that the Lord has to say (cf. Ps. 62:12).

To see the possibility of salvation, then, in the 'implanted word' is to see the possibility of total recreation. 'Look, I am making everything new' (Apoc. 21:5). It is to see the possibility of the new heaven and the new earth. These are the dimensions of that righteousness for which we have to hunger.

The trouble with the anger of man is that it is a defective response to a very real disorder; it is defective because it is not comprehensive enough. It does not include itself in the problem against which it reacts. It judges in a divisive way, pitting 'me' against the rest, or pitting part of me against the rest of me.

But God's new creation is not divisive. However hard it may be to hold to this belief without slipping into an untenable belief in the impossibility of damnation, it is important not to stress the possibility of damnation in such a way as to make nonsense of redemption. It is theologically and philosophically disastrous to envisage heaven and hell sitting side by side for ever, each bearing witness to the failure of the other.[6]

Damnation, however real a possibility, is unintelligible. It is a nonsense, which leaves the sense of heaven intact. There are no bits missing in heaven.[7] This is the truth in the controversial and difficult doctrine of *apocatastasis*[8]: we must safeguard the wholeness of God's vision of all that he has made, we must respect the complete efficacy of God's creating.

This is precisely the problem that puzzled Julian of Norwich, as she reflected on her 'showings of divine love'. In her vision of creation, 'I saw not sin',[9] and in all that she saw, she found only God's assurance of the eventual utter rightness of everything. Faithful to the Church's teaching, she confesses the possibility of damnation; but damnation does not enter into her vision of God's universe. She cannot see how it can be reconciled with the promise that 'all shall be well', and she gets no answer to her inquiry on the subject. The nearest she can get to any understanding of the matter is that 'there is no more mention made' of the devil and of the damned 'before God and all his holy ones'.[10] They constitute neither an embarrassing presence in heaven nor an aching absence, they simply do not enter into the picture at all. It is from the point of view of hell that hell is real, not from the point of view of heaven. And this is not a concession to sentimental squeamishness, it is due to a rigorous theological sense.

What mercy glimpses, then, is the whole world made new. It cannot consign any part of it to damnation, any more than God can be thought of as hating or dismissing anything that he has made. 'God did not make death,' as the Book of Wisdom boldly declares (1:13). It is intolerable to suppose—whatever difficulties we still have to face—that 'God saves' and 'God condemns' can be set side by side as two similar and parallel statements. God does not condemn, in the sense in which he can be said to save. God does not judge. As St John explains it, judgement is not any act of God; the judgement is simply that some people, unintelligibly, may prefer the darkness, after the light has come into the world (John 3:19). But in God all is light, and whatever comes into the light is light (cf. Eph. 5:13–14). In God there is no condemnation.

Therefore in us, too, there must be no condemnation. Our Lord's word, 'Do not judge" (Matt. 7:1), is absolute and final. No exceptions are allowed.

But this means that we must see the human race as a whole, without dividing it up into the good and the bad, or even the relatively better and less good (or worse and less bad). This is why our Lord refuses to endorse our comfortable division between those who murder and those who merely mutter (Matt. 5:21ff). We are all of us under the same condemnation (cf. Rom. 3:19), we are all of us in need of the same mercy. And it is only in the context of that totality that mercy is offered. We cannot try to secure renovation and forgiveness only for our particular corner of the world. Once again, it is all or nothing.

If we can see the world in this light, then surely our indignation in face of all the evil that we perceive must begin to shift. Instead of being a particularized anger at particular ills, it will tend to become a general, impersonal, refusal to accept anything other than the perfection intended by God. It therefore merges with our hunger and thirst for righteousness, and becomes an important part of our determination not to be fobbed off with anything less.

But this kind of anger cannot really be directed against any particular individuals, and it is at this point that anger really comes into its own, no longer as 'the anger of man', but as a participation in the very wrath of God.

According to the classic Christian ascetic tradition, it is always futile to squander our anger on one another. That is a waste of anger. Anger is made to be directed against the demonic, not against our fellow men and women,[11] its proper purpose is to give us energy to escape from the various ways in which we find ourselves a prey to the demonic in ourselves.[12] Anger should be our response to the whole situation of wrongness, in which we and everybody else are caught up from the very moment of our birth. It is the colossal repudiation pronounced by the new Adam in all his members of the dingy world produced by the sin of the first Adam. 'Let grace come and let this world pass.'[13]

But in this repudiation of a whole 'world', no man or woman is rejected. All men are, in principle, on the same side of this dichotomy. This is a judgement wrought by that Word which is sharper than any two-edged sword (Hebr. 4:12), which divides, not one man from another, but all men from that miasma of wrongness in which we are trapped. It separates a man from his sin, not from his neighbour. And what else is forgiveness, what else does mercy seek to do?

Mercy is no soft option. It is not a matter of conniving or finding excuses. It is the only really hard-headed response to evil, faced frankly and judged accurately for what it is. It is the only power which can face evil and not flinch, because it knows a power stronger than evil, the power of God's Word, in which the promise of creation still stands, and in which, therefore, the seed of new creation waits to germinate.

This then is the true righteous indignation. It is a refusal to make do with this shoddy world of sin. But that in no way involves any dissociation of ourselves from that world of sin. The world we repudiate is the world of which we are a part. Our merely human indignation is simply another symptom of the wrongness of things. Our inability to be effectively friendly towards those who have hurt us is just another sign that we and they are all tangled up in the same web of wretchedness. Even if it makes it impossible for us sometimes to live in the same house or even the same land as some of our brethren—just as Paul and Barnabas had to put many miles between them (Acts 15:39)—it is nevertheless a bond between us. The wound which hurts us and the hurt which prevents reconciliation are both but different ways of sharing in the same lump of sin, and so constitute the same need for mercy. We are at one even in being divided by sin, and we must insist valiantly on not accepting the division as having the last word. The seed of new creation is the ground of our hope, even when nothing can be seen except the frost of the decrepit world of sin. And in that hope we are again united.

Forgiveness is, therefore, not essentially a matter of feeling benign towards those who offend us, or those whose deeds offend us. The feeling of friendship may or may not be possible, depending on temperament and so on. The more sensitive we are, the less likely it is that reconciliation in any consciously intimate sense will be possible.

But forgiveness is not that, it is the dogged refusal to settle down in such a world of discord. Forgiveness is the hunger and thirst for total rightness which repudiates with grim determination this world in which we cannot be perfect.

90

It is, perhaps surprisingly, this grim refusal which is the matrix of true compassion, true sympathy. Anything less than this will yield only a sentimental and fragile substitute. This is not to say that there is nothing good in more partial, emotional kinds of sympathy. The natural response of fellow-feeling to somebody in distress is a good one, so far as it goes, like any other instinct of friendship. But truly supernatural charity has to go further, and it is in the context of supernatural charity that our natural affections come into their own perfection and purity. Mere fellow-feeling has to look for some basis for itself; charity needs no basis except God. And when we are dealing with mercy, especially that most typical mercy which we call forgiveness, we are dealing with a kind of love which has, indeed, no basis except God.

It may seem rather a comedown to move from reflections like these to 'charity' in the sense of almsgiving. But we cannot leave this beatitude without a brief reflection on almsgiving. The very word 'alms' recalls us to 'mercy', deriving as it does from the Greek word for mercy (*eleemosyne*), and almsgiving was regarded in the time of our Lord as a specially typical act of mercy, and in particular it was regarded as a way of atoning for one's sins, and so was closely connected with the mercy that men hope to receive from God.[14]

This must not be taken to suggest that we can somehow bribe our way into God's mercy; it is not the same thing as 'conscience money'.

The reason why almsgiving is a remedy for sin is that it is a way of restoring likeness to God. And it is like God because it is reckless. The rule that our Lord gives is absolutely clear and unambiguous: 'Give to everyone who asks' (Luke 6:30). He does not say that we should find out what they are going to do with it, he does not say that we should make sure that they are not alcoholics, nor does he give us any way of protecting ourselves against being exploited by people who are perfectly capable of supporting themselves.[15] All the normal prudential limitations we set upon our generosity are conspicuous by their absence from our Lord's teaching. We like to think that we are being 'responsible' in not giving to everyone who asks. But maybe it is arrogant and even ungodly to want to be responsible in this kind of way.

When our Lord tells us to be merciful as our heavenly Father is merciful, he prefaces this command with the declaration that God gives to good and bad alike with no distinctions (Luke 6:35f). He is, if you like, irresponsible in his giving. He does not wait to see whether we are going to make good use of his gifts before he gives them; his grace is not given strictly in accordance with how he foresees we shall profit by it.[16] He rains upon the just and the unjust in equal measure, regardless of whether or not the unjust hath the just's umbrella. God gives abundantly to all and sundry, without stint, without calculation. Clement of Alexandria is doing no more than underlining the teaching of Christ when he says, 'Give to everyone who asks you, for truly this is the way that God loves to give.'[17]

It is in this spirit also that God forgives. Forgiveness is only a special instance of the way in which God manages all his giving. He does not say, 'Well, all right; you're a good chap underneath, I'll give you one more chance.' When St Peter wanted to make sure he had got the arithmetic of forgiveness right, he was answered only with a sum he probably did not know how to do (Matt. 18:22). Forgiveness is reckless. It squanders itself upon rogues who have no intention of improving themselves. All it asks for is that it be received. The only unforgivable sin is the sin against forgiveness, the sin which directly and immediately refuses forgiveness.

Now it is in this spirit that forgiveness must be received too. We must enter into the spirit of it, and that is the Holy Spirit, God's Spirit poured out into all the world. We must not try to pretend that somehow we are forgivable and that that is why we are forgiven. We are no more and no less forgivable than anyone else. If we try to privilege our claim to forgiveness, it is not forgiveness we are looking for, but some other kind of recognition. If it is truly forgiveness we are after, then it must be unconditional and unlimited forgiveness. And we can receive that only if we are prepared to accept the company that forgiveness places us in. It is no good wanting to be forgiven and then reserving the right to look round disapprovingly on all the other fellows.

This is why forgiving is so inseparable from being forgiven. And reckless almsgiving, such as our Lord recommends, is surely a singularly apt expression of the spirit of forgiveness. It is a way of acting out a whole way of seeing the world that is quite different from our normal, calculating approach. There may be many benefits we can convey to our fellow human beings in more calculating ways; but if they exhaust our repertoire it may be that the most important act of all is missing.

Of course we shall fall short of the ideal of giving to everyone who asks. But we should admit that this is simply a further evidence of our share in all that is wrong with the world, and not disguise it with pretensions of 'responsible giving'. We will sometimes not give because we cannot be bothered, or we are afraid of the consequences, or because the particular beggar stinks, or because he speaks rudely to us, or because he behaves like a con man, or because he has annoyed us in the past. There are a thousand and one reasons why we will sometimes not give, but they are bad reasons. And so long as we know that they are bad reasons, they will probably not do much damage. They will be simply part of the brokenness which we entrust, in hope, into the hands of God. But when bad reasons become good reasons, then we are moving out of the sphere of mercy, and shifting back into the world of our own making and planning. And in that world there is no 'implanted word' which can save our souls.

Chapter Ten

Blessed are the pure in heart,
for they will see God.

This beatitude directs our attention to the heart. A modern reader
is liable to misunderstand this, because for him 'heart' will almost
certainly suggest 'the seat of the emotions', contrasted, as likely as
not, with 'head', taken to be the seat of thought. But the ancient
world, whether we are thinking of Semitic peoples or Greeks and
Romans, made different connexions between parts of the body and
psychological functions. The Hebrews allocated different emotions
to different parts of the body, but not to the heart in particular.
Anger was situated in the nose, presumably because people snort
when they are angry; compassion was situated in the bowels. The
heart was taken more generally to stand for the 'inner man', and in
particular for the mind and the will. The Greek word used in the
New Testament has a similar range. Our beatitude does not, then,
refer to the heart as the seat of the emotions, but to the whole
interiority of human consciousness and activity. The heart is a
symbol of what we are in ourselves, of the source of all our reactions
and aspirations. 'Blessed are the pure in heart' will mean something
like 'Blessed are those who have a pure source of life in them.'

The letter of St James, as we have seen, suggests that there is in
us a kind of built-in law, a word, as he says, planted in us, which
is our own law of truth and therefore of freedom. 'Heart' in our
beatitude refers to something like this. Blessed are those whose
inner principle is pure, unmuddied.

Our Lord is very insistent that his kind of morality concerns the
heart. He is not satisfied with any merely external morality. It does
not impress him that we should just manage to behave ourselves

94

properly, he is not prepared to get excited about any observance of external purity, such as that of the Pharisees with all their washing of pots and pans and hands (Mark 7:3f). For him the important thing is that it is from the heart that good and evil proceed. If the heart is evil, then however many pots and pans we wash, however often we wash our hands, we are unclean.

We have somehow got to get inside and unmuddy the source of life.

A very important factor here is what we may call Christian spontaneity. It does not, perhaps, in the last analysis, matter all that much what you do with forethought; what really matters, what is really revealing, is what you do without thinking, what you do if you are woken up suddenly in the night, what you do when you do not have time to work out how to respond. It is this that will reveal what kind of person you are, and that is what is important. After all, the kingdom of heaven comes like a thief in the night (1 Thess. 5:2), with a suddenness which will not allow us to work out how we are going to react.

The way the tree falls, so will it lie (Eccles. 11:3). The way that it falls is certainly the result of a long process; but its actual falling is a crisis that comes suddenly. There is quite a lot we can do in advance to determine how we shall fall, but all of it is but rehearsal for something we shall have to do instinctively when the time comes. This is why it is so important to take seriously St Thomas' refusal to identify virtue with mere right action; so long as we have wrong desires, even if we do not give in to them, we are not yet virtuous.[1] When it comes to the final crunch, there may not be time not to give in to them, there may be no opportunity for second thoughts. When someone offends us, maybe our immediate reaction is, 'I'll get him!', and then we realize and tick ourselves off. But eternity may break in before we have reached the second stage in the process.

We must unmuddy the very source of our reactions, so that our spontaneity itself is transformed.

This can only come about through the Holy Spirit. He is given to us by God to be in us a source of living water, welling up from our own hearts (cf. John 7:38). It is important to be clear about this. There has been for centuries far too much readiness to make a sharp separation between the natural and the supernatural, with the result that we tend to look for manifestations of the Spirit that can be experienced precisely as not coming from within ourselves. 'Is it God or is it me?' is the question we sometimes ask. But it is a nonsensical question, if we mean it seriously. The essential question is not whether it is God or me, but whether it is God or Satan. It is Satan who comes to us as an outsider, who works on us externally, and can get possession of us only by constraining us. But God works within us, within our hearts and minds, within our freedom.[2] It is from our own hearts that the living water of the Spirit comes bubbling up. (Actually the Greek text says 'belly'. The Hebrew word which may well underlie the Greek here can cover pretty well all that is inside us, including womb as well as belly; the point is that it is from *inside* that the water flows.)

It is from within us, deep down within us, that the new life proceeds, and that means that anything which is not an expression of us will not be an expression of God either.

But in some sense the converse of this is also true. What is not an expression of God will not be a true expression of us. Man is made to reflect the image and likeness of God, and it is that image and likeness which is restored by grace, by the working of the Holy Spirit. Purity of heart is not just a matter of our own interiority. Our Lord said to his disciples, 'You are pure because of the word which I have spoken to you' (John 15:3). If we have a clean heart, it is because God has given us a clean heart. The water welling up in us unto everlasting life is the water that proceeds from the Father and the Son. It is God dwelling in us who gives us a true interiority that is genuinely ours, but is not simply our own.[3]

St Catherine, we are told, was at one time very devoted to the verse from Psalm 51, 'Create in me a clean heart'; and one day she had a strange experience in which it seemed that the Lord came to her and removed her physical heart. Later he inserted a new heart into her, his own heart, saying, 'I am giving you my heart so that you can go on living with it for ever.'[4]

Whatever else we may want to make of a story like this, it is at least a dramatic representation of the teaching of St Paul. 'I live now not I but Christ lives in me' (Gal. 2:20). Our deepest identity is Christ. It is because he lives in me that I can properly say 'I'.

Western man has come to be very conscious of identity, and often as a problem. He does not feel secure about his identity, and feels that as a grievance. In response to this, he generally tries to find ways of bolstering up his 'Ego', to reassure himself that he is something.

Eastern religions, by contrast, generally stress the 'Not-I', particularly Buddhism with its doctrine of non-self, *anatta*.[5]

Christianity insists on both. Our identity is 'I' and 'Not-I'. Life which is authentically mine must proceed from a truly personal centre which I can identify as 'mine'; it is a part of man's dignity, according to St Thomas, that he is the source of his own actions, just as God is the source of his own actions.[6] Our freedom is the created image of God's freedom.

But our created freedom can really subsist as such only if it is rooted in God's freedom. The essential source of my identity is God. Within my own interiority in myself is God's interiority in me; and, according to St Augustine, God is even more intimately within me than I am in myself.[7] There is really only one source of life in us, and that is fully human only in being also divine. God is the heart of our heart.

But this means that there is a mystery at the source of ourselves. If we are indeed truly the source of our own lives, we cannot expect to grasp or fathom that source. In Thomistic language, we cannot apprehend the essence of our own souls.[8] To have a pure heart is to have a heart that is known to be rooted in the mystery of God and which must therefore systematically elude our grasp.

The mystery of God and the mystery of the soul belong together; to the complaints of those who found the God of the Jews and the Christians too elusive to be convincing, Jewish and Christian apologists responded by reminding them that man too is just as elusive.[9] To the demand, 'Show me your God', Theophilus retorts, 'Show me your man and I will show you my God.'[10]

To have a pure heart is to have a life which wells up in us from a source too deep for us to plumb. To have a pure heart is to have a heart that is not just created by God and then abandoned to us for us to make the most of it; it is to have a heart which is constantly being created and sustained by the newness of the life of God. Meister Eckhart bids us go beyond the righteousness of calculated good works and become 'free and untrammelled as our Lord Jesus Christ is free and untrammelled, conceiving himself constantly anew, without any break, beyond time, from his heavenly Father.' In the same way we, too, should be without past and future, without

97

before and after, in each 'Now' bringing forth our good works in Christ, conceived from the Father.[11]

If we can unmuddy the source of life in us, if we can allow God to recreate us from deep within, so that there is a pure life in us, Christ's life as well as our own, then this must inevitably affect the way that we are and the way that we see. There is an interaction between seeing and being. The kind of person you are affects the kind of world that you see. For that matter, even the kind of mood you are in affects the kind of world you will see. When you are suffering from acute indigestion, the world is a very different place from what it is when you are feeling fine.

And conversely what you see affects what you are. If you see the world as a rather grim affair, you will become a grim person. If you see the world as a place where there are butterflies, you will probably be a rather more light-hearted kind of person.

If our life is rooted in God, so that the well-spring of life in us is God, then we shall see as God sees. And what God sees is God. This is why those who are pure of heart will see God. In one sense, God does not see anything but God. He does not have two different kinds of vision, one for seeing himself and another for seeing his creatures.[12] It is within his eternal and blissful contemplation of himself that he sees all that he has made. That is why he sees that it is very good.

If we have a pure heart, a source of life welling up from the eternity of God, then what we shall see is God. 'Everything is pure to the pure' (Titus 1:15). Those who have a pure heart cannot see evil, just as it is said of God that he is too pure to be able to see evil (Hab. 1:13). To have a pure heart means that wherever you look, whatever you are looking at, what you see is God. God, revealing himself in myriads of different ways, but always God.

We must not think of this in childish terms. It does not mean simply that when you look at butterflies, you get a syrupy feeling inside and say to yourself, 'How utterly beatific!'. It means that you are going to have to look at a man on a cross, broken, his wounds streaming with blood, and know that you are looking at God. To have a pure heart is to be capable of that.

Certainly part of our discipline towards that is to learn to look at butterflies. According to one important tradition in the early church the first result of purity of heart is that it becomes possible for us

98

to resume our original human task of looking at things.[13] Evagrius quite clearly regards 'physics' (the contemplative understanding of nature) as a necessary stage between the ascetic goal of purity of heart[14] and the final goal of contemplation of God,[15] and this seems to be the view of Origen, too.[16] The Gospel of Thomas says, 'Know what is before your eyes and what is hidden from you will be revealed to you,' which Ménard connects with Clement of Alexandria's reference to the view that philosophy begins with 'wondering at what is there'.[17] Cyril of Jerusalem, commenting on the way in which we come to know God by considering his works, makes the adequacy of our conception of his greatness depend on the greatness of our contemplation of his creatures.[18] Similarly in Origen's view, it is in learning how to see things properly that we first begin to be enchanted by the beauty of God.[19] This visible world is the appointed 'schoolroom of rational souls, where they learn to know God', being led by the things that can be seen to an awareness of what cannot be seen.[20]

And learning how to see things is very much a matter of learning how to 'wonder intelligently'.[21] As St Basil, for instance, presents it, it is essentially learning how to respond to the elusiveness and mysteriousness of things.[22] If purity of heart means recognizing a mystery within ourselves, it leads us also to confront the related mystery that there is in all other created things.

St Basil is quite confident that the more we know about things, the more we shall be confronted with this mystery. He is not afraid of science.[23] The more thoroughly you inform yourself about things, the more you will find to wonder at; the more you will realize that you cannot get to the bottom even of created things.

This is, of course, poles apart from the position of Aristotle. In his view, wonder arises out of man's natural desire to know and to understand things. When he runs into something he does not understand, he wonders; this makes him investigate and study whatever it may be, until he has understood it. But then, evidently, he stops wondering.[24] Wonder as an integral part of the good life is not something Aristotle would approve of.[25]

St Thomas refers to Aristotle for the view that wonder is the beginning of wisdom; but in his view wonder is not merely an irritation, it has its own proper delight.[26] And this is surely not unconnected with the paradox to which Josef Pieper has drawn our attention:[27] on the one hand, St Thomas declares that 'the intellect penetrates to the very essence of a thing';[28] but he also says that 'the essential principles of things are not known to us'[29]. Pieper shows how these two apparently contradictory propositions can be reconciled: it is the doctrine of creation which unites them. Things are knowable and intelligible precisely because they proceed from a mind, the mind of God. But this at the same time constitutes their unfathomable mysteriousness. When we get to the bottom of things, reaching their very essence with our minds, what we find there is the inscrutable mystery of God's creative act. We can indeed know the essence of things, but what we 'know' is, in another sense, totally beyond us. Really to know something is to find ourselves tipped headlong into a wonder far surpassing mere curiosity. This is the 'rational wonder' to which natural contemplation leads us, and it is the first stage of the ascent to the final and utterly transcendent mystery of the One, the highest God, who can be known only by a mind that has reached the limits of its comprehension and then, in love and faith, launched out into the silence beyond.

But it is not only the beauty and order and fascinating mysteriousness of nature that lead us through the world of *visibilia* to the *invisibilia Dei* (cf. Rom 1:20). The darker, more frightening or depressing *visibilia*, too, have to be faced.

In Christian thought, the elimination of the 'passions', which means the purging out of all alien elements that have somehow found their way into our hearts, leads towards the restoration of the kind of innocence that Adam and Eve had before the fall. This is a theme which is richly developed in some early Christian literature, but there is only one aspect of it which need concern us here: the restoration of innocence, of inner wholeness and purity, means that we need no longer be shy.[30] Since the fall, man is an embarrassed animal, quick to hide, generally capable of overcoming his timidity only by arrogance and bluster. But man restored no longer has a 'spirit of timidity' (2 Tim. 1:7). He is not afraid to look anything in the face. He is not afraid of beauty or of being attracted by it.[31] Nor is he afraid of things which are normally regarded as ugly. He can look anything in the face, even sin.

There is an interesting connexion made in one of the sayings of abba Poemen between purity and our attitude to sin:

100

Abba Poemen said that if a man attains to what the apostle says, 'Everything is pure to those who are pure,' then he sees himself as less than the whole creation. A brother said to him, 'How can I consider myself inferior to a murderer?' The old man said, 'If a man attains to this word, should he actually see a man committing murder, he would say, "This man has committed only this one sin, but I commit murder every day." '[32]

Purity of heart clarifies things, so that we can be humble in our view of others, seeing them as good, not as sinners, as essentially good even in their occasional sins. But more importantly it clarifies things so that we can see even sin in the context of a whole vision of God and of his providence and his creation. Guigo I in several of his *Pensées* calls us to be compassionate towards sinners, and he derives this compassion from a clear perception that a man, in himself, is good and therefore admirable, it is only his defects which are evil; and his defects do him so much more harm than they do anyone else, that the proper response is to be compassionate, not indignant.[33]

But maybe we have to go even further than that. Purity of heart makes us sensitive to the good that is truly present even in what is evil. Thus the pseudo-Dionysius, in his chapter on love, reminds us that it is inconceivable that anything or anybody should be totally devoid of good. He takes the example of a sex-maniac. His desire is irrational and wrong; but nevertheless, in so far as what he is looking for is some kind of dim reflection of genuine union and friendship, he has some part in goodness. Even a person who opts for the worst possible kind of life is at least desiring life and the life that seems best to him and, so far as it goes, that is good.[34] The pseudo-Dionysius is inviting us to see evil as being only a distortion within something which is far more essentially good, as being, therefore, in some sense, a genuine, if misguided, aspiration towards good.

In his hymn on the woman who was a sinner, Romanos the Melodist delicately insinuates that it is Christ who can truly give her what she had been looking for in vain with all her previous lovers. If the discontinuity involved in conversion is important, so also is the continuity. The unchaste love was an abortive experiment in loving; it is essentially the same experiment that now succeeds with Christ.[35]

St Thérèse of Lisieux in her autobiography says that it was precisely the greed which made her, as a child, say, 'I'll have the lot!' when asked to select a toy from a gift box, that motivated her aspiration towards total sanctity.[36] The bad quality is not suppressed, it is converted to become the backbone of her sanctity.

And even with all its deficiencies, sin itself can be put to work by God; granted that it happens, it at once begins to function as part of the providential ordering of all things for our good. This is true even of our own sins.[37] To be humbled by our sins is, in the long run, far more profitable for us than for us to become conceited because of our moral success.[38]

After all, consider again the cross of Christ. There we see the supreme revelation of the destructiveness and wickedness of men. Yet there, too, we see the supreme revelation of the love of God. To have a pure heart, then, is to be able to look sin in the face, whether it be our own or that of others, and see there not only sin, but God.

In Christ everything is 'Yes', there is no 'No' (2 Cor. 1:19). Our forlorn condition after the fall is that we are indeed condemned to know good and evil, and to know good all too readily only by contrast with evil. It is often easier for us to define goodness as that which is not evil than to see it as being anything in itself.

But in God there is no darkness at all (1 John 1:5). God does not see good and evil, as it were, sitting side by side, and choose between them. God sees all that he has made, and it is very good (Gen. 1:31).

It is fatally easy for us to let go of a strong monotheistic conviction and effectively make Satan into an evil anti-god, and interpret our world in terms of two warring principles, pitted against each other till the end of time. This may sometimes be a picture which helps us, but we must realize that it would be very misleading if it led us seriously to suppose that there is any principle of evil which is actually on a level with God. Evil is, in the last analysis, not an independent power which can challenge God; it has no true being of its own. It is a mystery of evil which somehow arises as a weakness within the good which God has made, a surd which is strictly incalculable, which can never be reckoned up over against the good. Behind the good there is everything, there is God; but behind the evil there is nothing. As St Thomas says, evil, as such, strictly speaking, has no cause.[39] It is irrational and incomprehensible. It is not something you 'have to reckon with'; you cannot reckon with it. It is a nonsense. If you really penetrate to the heart of anything that shows itself as evil, the only true being you will ever find there is good. There *is* nothing else. *Ens et bonum convertuntur.* If you insist on finding a real cause of what is evil, the only cause you can find is God.[40]

If we unmuddy the well-spring of life in us, what we shall see is God, always God; we must become able, as Meister Eckhart tells us, to burrow through any situation in which we find ourselves, any situation which confronts us, and discover God there.[41] There is no reason for us to be fastidious or dismayed. God is everywhere. To have a heart that is pure is to renounce choosiness, it is to find the courage to look anything in the face, however unattractive it may appear to be, and know, 'Here too is God.' The light shines in the darkness, and the darkness cannot begin to defeat it (cf. John 1:5).

It is a mistake to think that our way to heaven is best negotiated with blinkers on. Custody of the eyes may sometimes be a sensible prudential tactic, but it is a doubtful philosophy of life. We shall not see God the more clearly for narrowing our vision.

Purity of heart clarifies vision. It is the very antithesis of the cynicism of worldly wisdom. Where cynicism sees through all that is beautiful and good and simple, to find murkiness within, purity of heart sees through ugliness and sin and pain and failure to find God within.

It is also the antithesis of a kind of 'innocence' whose main concern is to keep out of mischief and to avoid having to face up to anything nasty. Rollo May says that we must distinguish between two kinds of innocence:

> One is innocence as a quality of imagination, the innocence of the poet or artist. It is the preservation of childlike clarity in adulthood. Everything has a freshness, a purity, newness and colour. From this innocence spring awe and wonder. It leads toward spirituality. . . .
> There is another kind of innocence, already hinted at in Melville's novella *Billy Budd, Foretopman.* Billy's type of innocence is that which does not lead to spirituality but rather consists of blinders—*Pseudoinnocence*, in other words. Capitalizing on naïveté, it consists of a childhood that is never outgrown, a kind of fixation on the past. . . . When we face questions too big and too horrendous to contemplate, such as the drop-

ping of the atomic bomb, we tend to shrink into this kind of innocence and make a virtue of powerlessness, weakness, and helplessness. This pseudoinnocence leads to utopianism; we do not then need to see the real dangers. With unconscious purpose we close our eyes to reality and persuade ourselves that we have escaped it. This kind of innocence does not make things bright and clear, as does the first kind; it only makes them seem simple and easy. It wilts before our complicity with evil. It is this innocence that cannot come to terms with the destructiveness in one's self or others; and hence, as with Billy Budd, it actually becomes self-destructive. Innocence that cannot include the daimonic becomes evil.[42]

It is interesting to compare with these words of a modern psychologist Meister Eckhart's fascinating re-interpretation of the story of Martha and Mary. Contrary to the normal view which takes Mary to be the type of the more advanced, contemplative soul over against the harassed and distracted Martha,[43] Eckhart takes Martha as the type of the mature Christian. And she is worried about her sister, afraid that she is just wallowing in sentimental devotion instead of getting up and maturing in the tussles of real life. Christ re-assures her that Mary is all right, she too has chosen the best part, but she is not yet very far advanced in it.[44]

According to St Anthony, 'No one can enter the kingdom of heaven without being tested; it says, take away temptations and no one will be saved.'[45] And the tradition of the Desert Fathers recommended that at least mature monks should not try to drive away their temptations at once, but should rather let them in and fight them that way.[46] It is out of all that goes on in us, including the real possibilities for sin, that our salvation is wrought. To avoid evil at all costs is to reduce also our capacity for genuine goodness.

If we are to have a purity of heart which makes it possible for us truly to see, to be visionary—and 'in the absence of vision, the people goes to the dogs' (Prov. 29.18)—we must ensure that it is a purity which is entirely 'Yes' in Christ, not 'Yes and no'. It must be a purity which fears no enemies because it has taken them into itself. As Rollo May says, realistically, 'Trying to be good all the time will make one not into an ethical giant, but into a prig. We should grow, rather, towards greater sensitivity to *both* evil and good. The moral life is a dialectic between good and evil.'[47] It is, paradoxically, the acceptance into our picture of ourselves of all the seeds of violence and disorder that will make possible a true wholeness of heart. Perfection, in so far as it is attainable in this life, is curiously dependent on a readiness to be imperfect. 'How happy I am', to go back to St Thérèse's exclamation, 'to find myself so imperfect at the time of my death.'[48]

If we will not attempt this, we shall be in danger of producing a religion and a morality which is intolerable to the truly religious, spiritual soul. At least a part of the move in the past hundred years or so to repudiate Christianity has been caused by the trivialization of Christianity by its reduction to what May calls 'moral calisthenics'.[49] Our aspirations, however worthy, have become worldly, yielding only a worldly vision. Against this, visionary artists have found themselves driven to protest. A morality which is too well adapted to the conditions of life in this world lacks the transcendence which alone can really appeal to the depths of our hearts and minds.[50]

An interesting example is the French poet, Rimbaud. His remarkably short youthful career as a poet has had a profound effect, including a profound religious effect. Paul Claudel declared that he owed his return to Catholicism entirely to him;[51] he was also an important influence on Daniel-Rops.[52] Yet he himself remained in profound rebellion against Christianity until his death-bed.[53] He sought illumination by a systematic exploration of evil:

> It is necessary to be a *seer*, to make oneself a seer. The poet makes himself a seer by a long, huge, calculated disordering of all his senses (*dérèglement de tous les sens*). Every form of love, of suffering, of folly; he himself seeks out and drains in himself every poison, to retain only its quintessence. Unspeakable torture, in which he needs complete faith, every superhuman power, in which he becomes the sickest of all men, the greatest criminal, the one most accursed—and the supreme Knower!—For he reaches the *unknown*! . . . He reaches the unknown and when, driven mad, he ends by losing the understanding of his visions, he has still seen them![54]

The poems which so inspired Claudel, high, mystical poems that they are, were composed at a time when he was living a life of utter degradation. When he came to renounce this life, he found himself constrained, at least if Enid Starkie's presentation is correct, to renounce also his quest for God.[55] He could not bring himself to subject himself to the pettiness and, in another sense, the degradation, of the religion of his childhood.

Where the known, the ordered, the understood, the civilized have all been tamed to become no more than a part of civic decency, the visionary must explore the unknown, the disordered, the unintelligible and the savage. If he is to see God he must by hook or by crook, break through to some *new* vision.

> . . . We desire to plunge
> To the depths of the abyss, whether heaven or hell, who cares?
> To the depths of the Unknown, to find something *new*![56]

The artist, as May suggests, is the rebel par excellence.[57] And it is part of his rebellious vision to be incapable of simply leaving anyone or anything in the role of 'enemy'.[58] The newness of his vision is nourished by the inclusion of what others discard.

It would be difficult, not to say impossible, to provide a Christian justification for the whole programme of deliberate degradation expounded by Rimbaud. But it would be irresponsible not to heed the warning. Our 'goodness' may be more compromised than our 'wickedness'. It may only be possible for us to reach any true integrity of heart and any authentic vision of God and of his truth by taking the advice of abba Poemen and letting go a little of our righteousness.[59] If we try to love God only with our good impulse, leaving the evil impulse out of account, at best we shall have a limping spirituality.

> God give me the strength and the courage
> To contemplate my heart and my body without disgust.[60]

This prayer of Baudelaire's curiously and presumably unconsciously echoes an old Christian prayer: 'Unveil our eyes, give us confidence, do not let us be ashamed or embarrassed, do not let us despise ourselves.'[61] The opening of our eyes should go with a more total acceptance of God's world, even as it is now, still incomplete, still in the making; and part of that acceptance is the acceptance of ourselves in our totality. Nothing less than this totality can sustain the integrity which should ultimately be ours.

We have come, I fear, to think of purity as rather a grim kind of affair, requiring constant alertness and defensiveness. But in a strange text found in the *Miscellanies* ascribed to Hugh of St Victor, we find purity of conscience represented as the soul's pillow, which helps to make its bed comfortable for it to sleep in.[62] This idea is probably to be linked with the allegorical monastery of Hugh of Fouilloy, who treats conscience as the soul's bed.[63] Purity of conscience, then, is a restful thing, it is like coming home and putting your feet up at the end of the day's work. After all the hard work of sin, we are invited to rest in purity. 'Rest from sinning', as it says in the Vulgate translation of Isaiah (1:16). Certainly this means resting in obedience, but obedience to God is simply obedience to the truth, the real truth, of what we are. It is the end of strain, even if it is not the end of struggle and of agony. The strain, the impurity, come from the refusal to acknowledge what is in us, the determination to treat ourselves as tame pets, instead of seeing that we are ruffians like the rest.

The acid question, perhaps, is what we are really aiming at. If all we are aiming at is a placid decency and competence in living, we should do well not to look too closely at things. But we are called to the vision of *God*. And are we really interested in God? St Thomas, apparently, when he was only five years old, started bothering his teacher with the question, 'What is God?'[64] In later life he told Christ that all that he wanted was Him.[65] But I wonder, if we were to stop people at random in the street and ask them what they wanted most, how many of them would say that they wanted to see God.

It is a measure of how far we are from purity of heart and from our natural condition that it should seem almost unnatural to us to be concerned with God. It is all too understandable that the old definition of prayer as the 'rising of the mind to God'[66] should have come to be mistranslated as the 'raising of the mind to God', and that the old liturgical exclamation, 'Up hearts!' should have become 'Lift up your hearts'. It barely even occurs to us that that upward movement is natural to hearts. If we had real hearts, hearts purified of all that is not heart, they would gravitate towards God as naturally as ham to eggs.

It is a measure of our humanity that we should come to be fascinated by God, and then all our life will fall into place, all our faculties will function in the way God intended them to function, we can then also put up with an awful lot of tiresome things in life, because they pale into insignificance beside the wonder of God. In that light, even pain and failure and betrayal cease to matter too much. Even they can be seen to shine, when they are seen in God, because even they have been accepted by God as the price for union with our world.

Our human nature is indeed, as St Thomas, following St Augustine, dared to assert, *capax Dei*, it has room for God.[67] But it has room for God because it has an innate capacity, even a need, to transcend itself. It is the mystery in us, the unfathomable profundity which makes us ungraspable even to ourselves, which is capable of enfolding the mystery of God.

We may try to deny that we have this drive within us to transcend ourselves, but if we do we shall consign ourselves only to dullness and death. But if we allow it to affect us, we shall be laying ourselves open to the most dangerous and devastating force in existence. The urge that drives us to seek God is the same as the urge that drives us to smash things. The old psychologists were absolutely correct in the ambiguous role they ascribed to our power of anger. It is the power that smashes through limitations, leading us either to become visionaries or to become vandals. If we yield to our aspiration to the vision of God, we must accept at the same time the possibility of our being vandals. Both, in different ways, are passionately dissatisfied with mere present reality.

This is the paradox of purity of heart. It is both peaceful and violent. It is peaceful because it is true. The strain of pretence is relaxed, our defences against our unwanted capacities are lowered, as they are in sleep. But what this allows to appear is an energy which cannot be contained. It is in fact the energy of nature and of order, but over against the order and 'nature' which are endorsed socially, it is likely to appear wild and unnatural. Rimbaud may have been wrong to pursue the unnatural in his quest for God, but he would have been even more wrong to deny his rejection of what was presented to him as being 'natural'.

Art is the alternative to violence.[68] Art creates order and peace by absorbing the power for violence and evil; violence, by contrast, arises, as likely as not, precisely from the attempt to cordon off violence and eliminate it. The violence must be sanctified, the poison distilled into pure energy. This is the alchemy which the

Christian is called to undertake.[69] This is the task of purity of heart. To have a pure heart is to enter into the very drama of God's creating. It is to have a heart like the heart of Christ, taking into itself all the anger and hatred of men and consuming them in and into a fire of infinite love.

Purity of heart is in fact one of the ways in which God actually makes himself present in our world. To have a pure heart is to become man renewed, man restored to his original calling and purpose. And man, in the image and likeness of God, shares in the creativity of his creator.

God sees all that he has made, and it is very good. It is good because he sees it, because he sees it as good. God's vision is not a response to beauty, it is its cause. In our own small way, we, too, create by our seeing, as we can sometimes discover in our moments of artistic creativity. The painter does not merely see and record a scene of beauty, he creates it. What he has seen is enriched by his seeing, it comes into its own in his vision of it.

The Christian is the artist in creation, the poet, the painter, the musician; and he knows this, he discovers his vocation in the world, when he comes to be haunted by a vision, a vision he has to express, but which yet constantly eludes his grasp. He has glimpsed something and it allows him no peace. Yet his only peace is in pursuing it. This is why artists are proverbially poor; their vision distracts them from prospering and becoming rich. And artists are also vulnerable: their vision distracts them from protecting themselves. To have seen is to be wide open, to be hopelessly undefended. And the artist, though he may be furiously angry at times, with himself and with everything else, is surely, in the end, a man who cannot simply condemn. His business is to look, not to judge.[70]

I am not saying that all Christians must become artists; most of us do not have the talent to paint or write poetry or compose music. Most religious art is atrocious. But we are all called to something not unlike the artist's way of life: to be haunted by something that will not let us go, to be dragged, almost unwillingly at times, in quest of a vision we have glimpsed. Because of this we must, we cannot help ourselves, we must take one more look at things, in case, in case. . . . We may be prudent men and women, able to make all kinds of calculations; but what we have seen cannot be confined within prudence and calculation. There is a power of life, of light, of beauty, of truth, welling up within us and almost forcing us to surrender ourselves to it, to become its vehicle of expression.

Blessed are the pure in heart, for they will not be able to imprison themselves finally in themselves. Even when they want only to be left alone in peace, they will find themselves responding to the call of the one they love.

> I was drowsy, but my heart was awake. Listen!
> My lover beats at the door.
>   'Sister my love,
> open and let me in
>   my dove, my perfection,
> my head is soaked with dew
>   hair drenched with the drops of night.'
> —'I am already undressed,
>   why should I get dressed again,
> I've washed my feet
>   and why should I get them dirty?'

> He took his hand off the bolted door
>   and my heart sank . . .
> I got up to let him in,
> my hands sticky with myrrh (Cant. 5:3–5)[71].

Chapter Eleven

Blessed are the peacemakers,
for they will be called sons of God.

There is an intimate connexion between this beatitude and the previous one, because purity of heart and peace belong inseparably together. True peace in ourselves is a product of purity of heart, and without true peace in ourselves we stand little chance of being peacemakers for anyone else.

There is a little story about this in the tales of the Desert Fathers:

> There were three friends who were eager workers, and one of them chose to devote himself to making peace between people who were fighting, in accordance with 'Blessed are the peacemakers'. The second chose to visit the sick. The third went off to live in tranquillity in the desert. The first toiled away at the quarrels of men, but could not resolve them all, and so, in discouragement, went to the one who was looking after the sick, and he found him flagging too, not succeeding in fulfilling the commandment. So the two of them agreed to go and visit the one who was living in the desert. They told him their difficulties and asked him to tell them what he had been able to do. He was silent for a time, then he poured water into a bowl and said to them, 'Look at the water.' It was all turbulent. A little later he told them to look at it again, and see how the water had settled down. When they looked at it, they saw their own faces as in a mirror. Then he said to them, 'In the same way a man who is living in the midst of men does not see his own sins because of all the disturbance, but if he becomes tranquil, especially in the desert, then he can see his own shortcomings.'[1]

This story not only suggests the impossibility of achieving anything much for anybody else until there is a modicum of peace in

111

ourselves, it also suggests what this peace involves. Peace does not come about through the more aggressive virtues, but through the more contemplative virtues, which allow truth to become apparent. Peace goes with an unflustered self-knowledge, which is won by such basic virtues as trust and humility rather than by more energetic pursuits.

Now it is quite impossible for there to be anything like this unflustered self-knowledge apart from the whole ambiance of mercy. Unless our vision is radically purified by mercy, we shall inevitably find ourselves being selective in what we are prepared to acknowledge as constituting ourselves. Instead of just seeing ourselves reflected in the still water of humility, we shall be agitating ourselves to try to produce a more pleasing image. But that way madness lies, not peace.

The way to peace is the acceptance of truth. Any bit of us that we refuse to accept will be our enemy, forcing us into defensive postures. And the discarded pieces of ourselves will rapidly find incarnation in those around us. Not all hostility is due to this, but it is one major factor in our inability to cope with other people, that they represent to us precisely those elements in ourselves which we have refused to acknowledge.

It is the whole truth alone which can support true peace. And the whole truth of ourselves is commanded and drawn into focus by the whole truth of God. 'Hear, Israel, the Lord our God, the Lord is one; and you shall love the Lord your God with all your heart and with all your soul and with all your strength' (Deut. 6:4f). Because God is one, he summons us to be one in our response to him, and it is for this that we are created. All that is in us finds its fulfilment in this integral love of the God who is one. This is how our hearts and minds and energies become one. And apart from this, there is no peace. 'No peace, says the Lord, for the wicked' (Isa. 48:22).

So it is in vain that we try to establish peace by superimposing some pattern of our own devising on the bits of ourselves that we are prepared to acknowledge. It is all that we are in very truth that must somehow or other be turned towards God in love, and in that already is the germ of peace.

But of course our human nature is fragmented and distorted. The truth of what we are existentially in ourselves is a broken truth.

112

And so our acquisition of peace involves redemption, it involves the cross.

According to the Vulgate text, in John 12:32 our Lord says, 'If I am lifted up from the earth, I shall draw all things to myself.' That is the magnetic pull that constitutes the dynamism of unity for the whole creation. There we find in our fallen world the love of God which is whole and can make us whole.

Christ is not just the model for us, 'he *is* our peace' (Eph. 2:14). He is the Single One in whom we become single.[2] He is the oneness of God expressed in human oneness; he is the One who comes forth from the One[3] to create and re-create oneness in us.

And so we discover something else very important about peace: it is not something that we can produce for ourselves, it is something that is given, that is proclaimed, by God in Christ. And it is given, proclaimed, in the first place, in the church. The peace which exists in God is a peace which now exists in us by virtue of its existence in the humanity of Christ. When we are baptized into his death on the cross, we are baptized into his peace, into his drawing of all things into unity.

In the ancient Christian burial places, the inscriptions frequently contain the phrase 'in peace (*in pace*)', and it is interesting that in some cases this does not mean 'May he rest in peace', but informs us that the person buried there lived and died 'in the peace of the church'. It means that the person was a Catholic.[4] It is not a statement of anybody's subjective condition, either past or hoped for; it is a statement of objective and verifiable fact.

We seem, then, to be dealing with peace in two rather different senses: there is the peace which we seek through self-knowledge, and the peace which is given objectively in Christ, to which we are united sacramentally in the church. But these are not really two different kinds of peace. The objective peace is the essential presupposition of our quest for peace. It is in Christ that our broken humanity is united with divine wholeness. It is because we are united with him in the peace of the church, that we can begin to accept the truth of our brokenness in self-knowledge. The peace that we seek is a wholeness that does not exist simply in ourselves, it is in Christ; but because it is in him, and we are in him, our acceptance of ourselves as we are, with all the upsets and tensions

113

consequent upon our sinfulness and the wretchedness of our world, can become less flustered.

To take up Meister Eckhart's paradox again, the spiritual man does not seek peace because he is not hampered by lack of peace. That is to say, it is not a subjective sensation of peace that is required; if we are in Christ, we can be in peace (*in pace*) and therefore unflustered even when we feel no peace.[5] For Meister Eckhart the equation 'in God = in peace' is always valid.[6]

There is an important psychological point here too, of course. If you strain too hard to be at peace, you will end up even less at peace than you were before. The beginning of peace must be acceptance of lack of peace, just as the beginning of relaxation must be acceptance of tension. If you are worried, nothing is gained by anxiously trying to get rid of worry. If you are worried, at least you should not compound it by being worried about being worried. If you are depressed, it is pointless to make it worse by getting depressed about being depressed. Recently Ionesco, even while complaining about persistent depression, declared, 'Nothing discourages me, not even discouragement.'[7]

We are told to cast all our care upon God (1 Pet. 5:7), which is not the same thing as trying to suppress all feelings of anxiety. The peace which is there in Christ is a peace which is for us, rather than strictly in us, and it is into that peace that we must plunge all our tensions and anxieties; the wholeness which is in Christ is the place where all the disorderly bits and pieces of ourselves are forged into unity.

Peace comes about through acceptance of truth; if we accept the truth of ourselves—the shifting truth of what we are from moment to moment—and constantly give it over into the truth of peace and wholeness in Christ, to which we have access in the church, then we shall be in fact in peace, whether or not we feel ourselves to be at peace. Peace is, then, something which enfolds us rather than something which we grasp. The peace which comes from God is a peace which 'surpasses all mind', all comprehension (Phil. 4:7). It is a peace which underlies, in Christ, all that we are, and in which, therefore, all that we are can come to rest and fulfilment.

But this peace is wrought on the cross. Our surrender to peace must often be, in the striking imagery of the *Cloud of Unknowing*, a matter of surrendering ourselves to God 'in the hands of our enemies'.[8]

We cannot have peace and at the same time be fastidious about our circumstances.

It is worth remarking in this connexion that in the gospels peace seems to be something that is declared authoritatively, rather than something which is worked out laboriously. Peace is not something negotiable; it is God's peace, the utter, invulnerable, tranquillity of his eternity, proclaimed into the world, proclaimed to us. Christ says to his apostles, 'I leave you peace' (John 14:27). And he sends them out to proclaim peace, 'Whatever house you enter, first of all say, "Peace to this house" ' (Luke 10:5). And this peace is so objective, almost solid, an entity that if there is no 'son of peace' in the house, the peace comes bouncing back upon the apostle, the preacher. The conventional greeting, *Shalôm* (peace), becomes now an authoritative declaration from the truth of God into the very depths of the human situation, piercing through all the psychological, emotional, political, social and other factors. Wherever there is a son of peace, God's word establishes officially a nucleus of peace. And surely we must go even further than that, and say that, since the passion, even where there is no son of peace, the word of peace is proclaimed. At the heart of the whole creation there is now a word, a crucified word, proclaiming peace to those who are far off as well as to those who are near (cf. Eph. 2:17), drawing into itself all the apparently incompatible factors which make up the human situation.

This is not unrelated to the authoritative word which is spoken in creation. Peace is being what you are, what you really are, what you are in God, what you are in obedience to the creative word of God, the 'implanted word' which is the law of your fredom.

To proclaim peace is to proclaim the re-creating power of God into the midst of a situation of disturbance and sin. Once we have begun, in Christ, in the church, to allow the implanted word to transform us into obedience, we can also begin to be peacemakers, speaking the divine, authoritative, word of peace to others.

But let us be quite clear what is involved in this. We are not told to negotiate. Negotiation may sometimes be a very excellent service, but it requires special talents, special position, and most of us will probably not very frequently be much use at it. But precisely as Christians, as the church, our task is quite different. It is to declare peace, the peace that exists in Christ and which therefore exists in the heart of mankind. And this is an essential part of the church's life. The church is, as the Vatican Council reminded us, the 'seed of unity' (*germen unitatis*),[9] in the world. But surely she is this because she is also the pillar of truth (1 Tim. 3:15). The peace which the church proclaims is the full unity of God's creation in the truth of itself.

To be a peacemaker is not, then, to come and patch things up, to arrange a settlement with balanced concessions all round, to try to find a compromise. It is to declare the truth of God and the truth of creation; it is to announce that a fallen world can be remade. It is to proclaim that the oneness of God has taken possession of the fragmented world of sin.

In this declaration there is no room for give and take, no room for concessions and compromise. The unity of God is the focus for everything that is real. Nothing has to be abandoned except falsehood. In Christ all the genuine aspirations and achievements of all creatures come to fulfilment. Nothing is left out.

The peace and unity which we must proclaim is, then, a rich and complex one, and the hope of such peace may seem paradoxical when we consider how incompatible some of the ingredients appear to be.

But this is the task which God has given to the church. As the *germen unitatis* her own very existence must be rich and complex and paradoxical, like the Word she must proclaim. Peace and unity are not to be achieved by paring down the complications of life, but by entering into the magnetic pull of God's unity. It is as God is one that creation is to be one. The unity of creation is as puzzling and elusive as the unity of God, and in it the truth of all that is is fully affirmed.

There is a startling text in Zechariah which has, so far as I know, played little part in Christian theology, but which is surely very suggestive for Christian trinitarian doctrine, 'The Lord will come to be king over all the earth, and on that day the Lord will be one and his name one' (14:9). The final oneness of God is presented here as a part of the final apocalyptic triumph of the Lord, and is inseparable from the gathering together of all creation under the rule of God in its definitive unity in worship. Maybe we ought to have more of this sense of triumph when we celebrate the feast of the Holy Trinity. The progressive disclosure of the Son of God and of the Holy Spirit which we celebrate throughout the cycle of feasts from Christmas to Pentecost seems to make it almost impossible to hold to the unity of God—and, in fact, it is almost impossible for most of us really to maintain the orthodox doctrine of God's Trinity in Unity without slipping unawares either into Sabellianism (one God dressing up as a diversity of persons) or into tritheism (three gods).[10] But the feast of the Holy Trinity is the triumphant celebration of the fact that God is One in spite of everything. Neither the diversity of his manifestation nor the threeness of the divine Persons makes him into three gods. And this paradox underpins the possibility of real, exhilarating unity in creation in spite of the immense, seemingly irreconcilable, diversity in its parts. The celebration of God's unity is the celebration of our own hope of total fulfilment, in which nothing is lost and nothing is left hanging without total integration into the whole.

We can get something of the feel of this kind of triumph from the way in which works of art contrive to harness together the disparate elements of which they are made up. We have perhaps lost the taste for the complexity which makes Elizabethan tragedies so obscure to modern audiences, but even our unsophisticated age needs a certain level of complication to stimulate its interest in a drama or novel, and even the most formless paintings or sculptures or compositions require a certain tension of improbability to be successful.

It is the unexpected harmonization of the seemingly irreconcilable which provides one of the most elemental thrills in a work of art, and something of the same kind is involved in God's triumph in creation.

And this is why truth can never finally be served or peace proclaimed by taking sides. In Christ, everything is 'Yes', it is not 'Yes and no'.

This is why heresy and schism are such dreadful and dangerous sins. They are failures to say 'Yes' in Christ. The heretic is one who chooses; this is what the word means. He is one who takes what he fancies and leaves the rest. And this is the absolute denial of the peace of God, the peace which is proclaimed in the catholicity of the church; it is the denial of the hope of re-creation.

This story used to be told about abba Agathon. Some people who had heard of his reputation for discernment wanted to test him to see if he

117

would lose his temper. So they came to him and said to him, 'So you are Agathon? We have been told that you are a fornicator and that you are conceited.' He replied, 'That is correct.' They went on, 'And you are Agathon the chatterbox and scandalmonger?' He said, 'I am.' Then they said, 'And you are Agathon the heretic?' And he replied, 'I am not a heretic.' They begged him, 'Tell us, why did you let us call you all these names without demur, but then refuse this last one?' He said, 'The things you mentioned first I ascribe to myself, because that is good for my soul. But being a heretic, that is separation from God, and I do not wish to be separated from God.' At this, they were amazed at his discernment and went away edified.[11]

To be a heretic is to set oneself at odds with God's affirmation of all that he has made, and so is to separate oneself from him in a far more serious way than in any other kind of sin.

Similarly disastrous is the sin of schism, which means taking sides, being partisan for one side of a dispute or one group of people *over against* some other. It is an attitude of 'Yes and no'.

The church is called 'Catholic', and this means that she is committed to saying 'Yes' to the totality of God's truth. She is the expression of that implanted word in which the whole world is to be made new. And so her task is not to choose or to take sides, but to find the 'Yes' that can be uttered in all the many situations and individuals that confront her in the world.

When Augustine was sent to preach the gospel in England, Pope Gregory evidently devoted a considerable amount of thought to this mission, and decided to advise the missionaries to try to salvage as much as they could of pagan buildings and ceremonies, while giving them a new Christian significance, so that the people would not be too badly shocked and bewildered.[12] This is surely the proper approach, concerned to affirm rather than simply to deny or contradict what is already there.

This is, obviously, not the same thing as simply endorsing every opinion uncritically. The church has, on occasion, uttered her anathemas against positions she regards as untrue. But her anathemas never mean that the church is defining itself over against the rejected proposition. It rejects the proposition because it is too small, too severely limited to serve the totality of God's truth; but this does not mean that the truth is to be found simply in asserting the opposite of the condemned formula. It is noteworthy that in the majority of dogmatic declarations, the anathemas are far more precisely worded than the positive teachings; and such precision as there is in the positive teaching is usually mysterious and expressed in formal language which is more like a rule for talking than a statement of belief. To tell us that Jesus Christ is fully God and fully man tells us very little in itself, but it gives us rules for a whole lot of language. It does not tell us what it means to be human, but it does tell us that any proposed definition of humanity must be applicable to Christ, for instance. It does not tell us what it means for Christ to be human, but it does tell us that his humanity cannot be defined as a case apart from our own.

The temptation, in any kind of controversy, is to harden our own position and emphasize its distance from the position of our opponents, and there is no doubt that Christians have often in fact argued this way. But the church as a whole can never rest content with such a procedure. St Paul himself sees a providential purpose in the existence of heresies (1 Cor. 11:19) and Origen, basing himself on this text, argues that the diversity of sects and heresies, far from discrediting Christianity, is a reason for taking it seriously. Any serious and useful undertaking produces a crop of different opinions and schools of thought, and it is from a careful scrutiny of all of them that a man becomes genuinely wise. Similarly the best way to be a wise Christian is to make a study of all the different philosophical and religious schools of thought, including the heretical sects.[13] An attentiveness to this kind of diversity makes us, in the long run, less likely to become sectarian and heretical ourselves. Even the opinions which we reject make their own contribution to our vision and understanding.

In the thirteenth century the church in the south of France was much harassed by heresy and schism, and the official Catholic mission to the region made little headway until a completely new style of apostolate was undertaken, first of all by Diego and his companion, Dominic, and later on by the sons of St Francis as well as the Dominicans. The startling thing about their new style was that it was, in many ways, indistinguishable from that of the heretics and schismatics. In order to make their disagreement with the heretics cogent, they had to learn how to agree with them where they could. And this was not just a pragmatic technique of persuasion; it came from a recognition that the heretics embodied something which was genuinely profitable for the church to adopt. In fact, the heretics and schismatics on the one hand, and the new religious orders springing up within Catholicism on the other, can all be seen to be responding to an essentially similar religious need and stimulus, as is well brought out in the classic study by H. Grundmann.[14]

This 'ecumenical' approach has been even more clearly stressed in the twentieth century, with the growing recognition that Christians of one church have to be prepared to accept a word of God addressed to them by other churches than their own. From a Catholic point of view, Karl Rahner wrote, in an essay first published in 1953:

> The convert [to Catholicism from another Christian church] is in many ways heir to a past which must be reckoned as Christian in a quite positive sense. Now this means that the convert ought to bring this inheritance with him into the common house of our Father, so that the church too can be the richer for it in Christian actualisation. Converts ought to be recognisable as having been Protestant. They should treat their inheritance not just as something past, but as something entrusted to them to give to their new church.[15]

Again, this does not mean that we should be so eirenic that we never venture to quarrel with anybody. It is often helpful to clarify our own understanding of things by having a fierce argument with somebody who disagrees with everything we are saying.

But, however fierce our arguments, we shall be failing as Catholics if we make our own views, our own attitudes, our own behaviour, the absolute criterion of acceptability. We must be prepared to insist on what we see to be true and to remind people of the evidence for our contentions, and this may often mean defending positions against proposed counter-suggestions; but we must not do this arrogantly, as if we were in full possession of the entire truth. We must hold on to what we see to be true, or even what we consider to be the most probable, as our contribution to the eventual discovery of all truth. But we must be fully prepared to find that such eventual discovery puts our little bit of truth in a light very different from that in which we ourselves saw it.

And we must likewise never simply dismiss the views of others, even if we are convinced that they are wrong. Even if we cannot see how they could ever be fitted into a synthesis with what we see to be true, we must allow for the possibility that there may be something there after all. In every evil there is a seed of good, in every untruth there is a thrust towards truth. Our 'Yes' must not, finally, be protected by any 'No'. We must seek to take sides with everyone and against no one, in the sense that we must seek to discover the implanted word wherever we look, and to declare the truth of it and so proclaim peace to it, the peace of God's unity and the wholeness of his creation.

If we prefer one opinion, one formula, to another, it should be because it is the one which is most capable of doing justice to all the others. According to Clement of Alexandria, the most reliable symptom of a true Catholic belief is that it is the most comprehensive.[16] A proposition P that can do justice to other propositions Q and R, while Q and R cannot do justice to each other or to P, is the one which is most likely to be in accordance with Christian truth.

But we must not be simplistic in our approach to peace. If this is the way in which we must proclaim peace, we may find ourselves getting into a painful and dangerous situation. This total peace is almost inevitably going to be in conflict with the partial 'peace' set up in the world. The peace which Christ gives to us is not 'peace by the world's standards', as we may perhaps interpret St John's phrase (14:27). The divine bringer of peace says of himself that he brings not peace but a sword (Matt. 10:34). His peace must dismantle the false and incomplete substitutes with which our fallen world abounds.

Just as the true scientist must allow his pet hypotheses to be destroyed by new evidence, so the world must be confronted with the new evidence of the gospel, challenging it to a peace far more comprehensive than anything it had ever dreamed of, a peace more total than it is even sure it would approve of. After all, this peace must include a reconciliation in creative mercy with all kinds of people of whom we do not approve. All our syntheses must be broken open again until at last our hearts and our vision are wide enough to contain the totality of God's gift.

Blessed are the peacemakers, for they will be called sons of God. And if sons, then heirs, heirs with Christ (Rom. 8:17). And Christ is the one to whom God has given everything, and nothing is to be snatched away. If we are peacemakers, we share in this total inheritance which belongs to Christ. All that the Father has he gives to the Son, even his own divine life. And we, in him, are called to be 'sharers in the divine nature' (2 Pet. 1:4). It is in this inconceivable sharing in God that all our created faculties find their contentment. All creation is reconciled and made perfect in 'becoming God' in its own way. This it is the church's task to proclaim; and in proclaiming it she is already blessed, because it gives her a true rooting in the bliss of God. But the crown of her fidelity to this task can come only at the end of time, when the new creation is disclosed in all its fullness. Because then she will see that peace which she has striven to proclaim established for ever in the new heaven and the new earth, and that totality of rightness will be for ever hers, in an inheritance that can never more be spoiled.

Chapter Twelve

Blessed are those who are persecuted because of righteousness,
for theirs is the kingdom of heaven.

Blessed are you, when they revile you and persecute you and speak all kinds
of evil against you, falsely, for my sake;
rejoice and jump for joy, for your reward is great in heaven,
for this is how they persecuted your predecessors among the prophets.

There is a clear tradition in the New Testament that the Jews,
God's people, could be relied on to persecute God's prophets (e.g.
Matt. 23:29ff, Acts 7:52). This constant infidelity came to a head in
their rejection of Jesus, who 'came to his own domain and his own
people did not receive him' (John 1:11). Our beatitude, with its
little appendix, seems to generalize the point. Assuming that the
sermon on the mount is addressed, in principle, to all believers, it
seems that all Christians are aligned with the prophets of old and
must accordingly expect to be persecuted, and they will be persecuted by an unspecified 'them'. But it is surely intended to be
significant that it is as prophets that they will incur this opposition
and hostility.

This provides a link with the preceding beatitude of the peacemakers. Christians are not primarily persecuted for being righteous
or for being followers of Christ, but for proclaiming righteousness,
for declaring Christ's word of peace, which, as we have seen,
involves breaking through the limited peace offered or at least
sought by factions and movements.

And this possibly suggests why we come round full circle in this
last beatitude, to echo the beatitude of the poor: theirs is the kingdom of heaven. In contrast to the aggressive, efficient methods of

human programmes and parties, the proclamation of God's peace seems to be curiously bankrupt and helpless. Wedded, as it must be, to God's total purpose and God's elusive methods, it seems, on the face of it, to have much less to offer to a world eager for results, than the schemes of those with less vision and more 'realism'. By comparison with the successes and the resources of the world, God and his preachers seem poor and ridiculous, but also slightly treacherous and subversive. But in their poverty and in the indignation they arouse they are truly serving the ultimate rule of God, precisely by refusing to operate simply on anyone else's terms.

The antinomy is presented starkly enough by St Paul. He regards his service of the Lord as being incompatible with 'pleasing men', let alone seeking to please men (Gal. 1:10). The hostility and persecution he inspires are, for him, evidence of his fidelity to God's word. If he were prepared to be more adaptable to what men wanted, he would not be in all the trouble he is in.

But it is not just a matter of how other people react to the proclamation of God's word of peace; the intentions and motives of the prophet himself are also concerned.

In St John's gospel, the Jews are said to be incapable of believing because they 'receive glory from one another' (5:44). There is, apparently, a radical incompatibility between human respect and belief in Christ. And the point here is surely not unlike the point being made in the beatitude of the poor, that human possession, even the possession of respectability, is too small. Our Lord declares about people who blow trumpets to attract attention to their good works that 'they have their reward'. We cannot expect to eat at both tables. If what we want is to get into the newspapers, very well, let us get into the newspapers; but then, we 'have our reward'. It is a short-term and practical objective, and once we have attained it, that is the end of the story.

But fidelity to God, loyal insistence on his word, his peace, his glory, is an objective which transcends such limited achievements. If we are not concerned to impress our fellow men and women, then there is a vaster reward in store for us, the reward of God's kingdom.

Of course, this does not mean that we must do all that is in our power not to get into the newspapers. A determination to avoid human respect and earthly fame at all costs is just as limited as a determination to acquire such things. And, in its own way, it is just as worldly and may even earn a kind of respect in the world.

What is so dreadful about the way of the Christian is that the believer in Christ can afford to be *indifferent*. 'I know how to be stuffed full, and I know how to be destitute,' says St Paul, 'I can cope with all of it in him who strengthens me' (Phil. 4:12f). This is the truly outrageous attitude. The world will perhaps respect us if we court it, it will perhaps respect us all the more if we sullenly disdain it; but it will hate us if we simply take no notice of what it thinks of us.

So, even though it is not the primary business of the believer to please men, it is equally not his business to go out of his way to displease men either. After all, to formulate one's own opinions simply on the basis of a need to disagree with someone else is still to take that someone else as the yardstick of truth. We do not become prophets simply because we go around being rude to and about everybody else. Prophets may often appear to be disagreeable, but disagreeableness, of itself, is not sufficient to make anyone into a prophet.

In fact, those who just want to be disagreeable 'have their reward' simply in being disagreeable and in seeing their disagreeableness provoking people to annoyance and hostility. The reward that our Lord promises to those who are persecuted for his sake is not intrinsic to the situation of persecution itself; he promises the peace of his Father's kingdom. Those whose highest enjoyment is battle for battle's sake will find little entertainment in heaven.

Christianity does not deliberately set out to shock. It shocks incidentally in simply being true to its own integrity. It is too big for the world. It cannot be reduced to any kind of worldly programme for social betterment or moral rearmament or intellectual advancement or artistic sensitization or spiritual renewal or whatever. It gathers up all such things, but puts them in a larger context which both relativizes them and pushes them further. This is why Christianity is an uncomfortable religion. It requires a head for heights and a taste for infinity.

This shows in the way in which Christian morals—and, therefore, Christian indignation too—differ from conventional morality and secular indignation. Christians, like anybody else, can feel indignant at the violence of terrorists and the excesses of the so-called per-

125

missive society; they can also share in people's anxieties about oppressive government and exploitation of poorer nations. But they also know that the shadiest and most unappealing elements in—or beyond the pale of—society, such as the prostitutes and imperial tax-collectors of the time of our Lord, may turn out to be much closer in fact to the kingdom of God than respectable, serious-minded, pious people like the Pharisees.

From her background, we should expect someone like Thérèse of Lisieux to be completely uncritical of conventional, middle-class Catholic values. Yet throughout her short life she showed herself aware of a deep sense of identification with such pariahs as murderers and atheists;[1] though she was aware that she was not herself guilty of very much in the way of sin, she declared that her approach to God would not be at all different if she had committed every sin in the book,[2] and this is evidently of a piece with her famous image of the two different ways that a doctor saves his children from harm: one falls over and hurts himself and is tended back to health by his father, but before the other one can fall over, the father removes the stumbling block. In Thérèse's view, there is no major gap, from the point of view of salvation, between the more or less innocent, like herself, and the thoroughly guilty.[3] In this she is, of course, being far more truly a typical Catholic than if she had simply accepted middle-class prejudices.

However much we may disapprove of terrorists, we must know also how to forgive, and that means to identify ourselves with them in God's mercy, not to be graciously condescending to them. We who mutter our resentments are, strictly speaking, in the same boat as those who express their frustrations in pointless and cruel violence (cf. Matt. 5:22).

However much we may disapprove of libertinism, we must beware of disowning it too naïvely. Christian chastity, too, requires a revolt against Victorian prudishness. The Church is not just there to sacralize primness, which is, in some ways, further from divine love than the fumbling, sick aspirations of the sex-maniac.

It is interesting that St Ephrem can refer to Christian chastity as being (from the devil's point of view) a 'misdemeanour' (he uses a Syriac root, *št'*, which is often used to refer to marital infidelity).[4] By the standards of our own day, too, there is something rather *naughty* about Christian sexual ethics.

It is a mark of a true Christian intellectual that he fits into none of the available slots. St Thomas, for instance, shocked both 'conservatives' and 'progressives', and even such modern 'conservatives' as, say, Cardinal Ottaviani, if allowed to be judged on what they have actually said and done rather than on what people assume they stand for, do not really fit the mould of the merely conservative. Consider Ottaviani's powerful stand against all modern methods of warfare, for instance.[5]

God is too big for this world, and those who are born of God are also too big for this world, and sooner or later the world will feel the strain of them. This world, in the sense of this world-order, ruled by the Prince of this world, is judged and found wanting by the Holy Spirit present in the church (cf. John 16:8). Even its virtues are, in themselves, unheavenly[6] and precisely because of their specious appearance they may be more serious an impediment to the progress of God's kingship than its more honest vices. Even its most honourable aspirations are not quite identical with those of the church.

From the point of view of the world, then, the church's very existence and the word which she speaks must seem to be, must actually be, seditious. And it is precisely this accusation which was brought against Christians by such serious-minded pagans as Celsus.[7]

And it is not just a matter of what Christians say and do; it is perhaps even more typically a matter of what Christians do not say and do. To use a venerable Christian image,[8] we habitually fail to turn up for duty. Christians are deserters, runaway slaves. The world and its master, the devil, expect us to clock in promptly at 7 am or whatever the appointed time is, but we have been 'seduced' by God, as Jeremiah complained (20:7).[9] We have been disabled by wrestling with mysterious heavenly visitations (cf. Gen. 32:24ff) and can only limp our way through the world.

One of St Ephrem's Christmas Hymns brings out vividly the shock that the coming of Christ is to worldly respectability and efficiency:

Come, rest and keep quiet in your mother's lap.
You are of noble birth and your forwardness is hardly fitting
for the sons of kings. You are David's son

127

and he was noble. And you are Mary's son and she
guarded her beauty in her secret room.

What sort of a baby are you, so merry and bright?
Beautiful child! Your mother is chaste, and your Father
the Hidden One whom not even seraphs can see.
What sort of a being are you?
Tell us, O son of the Merciful!

Feuding enemies who came to look at you
became merry and bright; they laughed together
and were at one with each other. Angry men became sweetened
through you and your gentleness. Who are you, child,
that even what is sour becomes sweet through you?

Who ever saw a baby so eager to meet
all who are near him? Tucked up in his mother's lap
he reaches out even to those who are far off.
What a beautiful sight, this child whose whole concern
is with everyman, that they all should see him.

Some came and saw you, bowed down with their cares,
and their cares fled away. And the brooder who came
forgot all his brooding. And the hungry forgot,
because of you, even his food. And men at their errands,
seduced by you, forgot where they were going.

Quieten yourself down, child, and leave us men
to get on with our business.[10]

It is important not to forget that 'worldliness' is a many-faceted
temptation for the Christian. We tend to think of it almost exclu-
sively in terms of luxuriousness and obvious vice. But these are not
the only snares laid for us by the world. In the synoptics' commen-
taries on the parable of the sower, the seed is threatened with
suffocation not only from the 'deceitfulness of wealth' and the
'pleasures of life', but also from 'worldly care' (Matt. 13:22 etc.),
and this is, in fact, mentioned first in all three texts. And 'worldly
care' covers all kinds of anxious responsibility in the world, including many things which would not normally be regarded as 'sinful',
and many which would perhaps generally be regarded as positively
virtuous.

And it is over against this last kind of worldliness that the primitive Christian tradition of *fuga mundi*, flight from the world, first grew up. In recent times there has been rather a reaction against the idea of flight from the world, but it would be unfortunate if we lost sight of the principle entirely. It is, no doubt, true that some kinds of flight have sometimes been practised which are unnecessary and inappropriate. But, properly speaking, flight from the world does not mean a panicky or mean-minded withdrawal from human concerns and interests, but a rejection of the narrowness and what we may call the puritanism of the world. The human heart is made for God and cannot really be content with less. And it is in God that the human heart finds its true joy in creatures. When St Paul expresses his personal longing to 'be dissolved and be with the Lord' (Phil. 1:23), he is not abandoning his concern for his fellow men and women, he is not forsaking the world like a rat deserting a sinking ship. It is only in the Lord that the world can find its fulfilment. It is the conceited and rather stuffy self-assurance of the world and its pretence of self-sufficiency that the Christian considers himself well rid of. It is because he has a higher and richer ambition for himself and for the world that he cannot take too seriously the demands that the world makes of him.

The original thrust behind the Christian *fuga mundi* was not a fearful hope to avoid temptation (in the ordinary, rather debased, sense of that word); it was not a fastidious attempt to escape from the impoverishment complained of by Thomas à Kempis as an inevitable concomitant of any traffic with men.[11] It was the fervour and generosity of their desire to serve God without any hindrance or distraction that led so many of the early Christians to renounce property and marriage, so that they could concentrate on 'pleasing the Lord' (cf. 1 Cor. 7:25ff). And out of this concentration came a readiness to engage in the Lord's task of proclaiming God's peace and furthering the work of his kingdom in ways which were often far more costly than the kind of mutual help normally offered by one man to another.

Flight from the world is inseparable from the insistence that we have only one Master, whose service is incompatible with any state of servitude to any other master. It is his will which governs our dealings with the world, and so we cannot accept that the world has any right to order us around. And if the world chooses to penalize us for this, that is a price we are prepared to pay.

That this is not meant to be just another kind of puritanism, a grim preferring of Christian duty to worldly entertainment, is surely suggested by the terms of our beatitude. When we find ourselves at odds with the world because of our fidelity to Christ, we are to 'rejoice and jump for joy', a reaction hardly compatible with stuffy dutifulness.

We must now turn our attention to a connexion between our Christian service and our being persecuted, which is even more intimate than any we have looked at so far.

The prophetic task of the church is to proclaim God's peace and his love into the actual situation of our broken and tormented world. And one of the most basic elements in our world, which we can see displayed in the psychology of many of our contemporaries, is that people are uncertain of themselves, uncertain that they are acceptable and lovable. This is why self-justification is such a typical activity of fallen man, and why the doctrine that we cannot justify ourselves is so essential to Christian belief.

As soon as we lose our nerve about ourselves, we begin to hide. Adam and Eve hid, and we have all, in one way or another, followed their example. We hide what we know or feel ourselves to be (which we assume to be unacceptable and unlovable) behind some kind of appearance which we hope will be more pleasing. We hide behind pretty faces which we put on for the benefit of our public. And in time we may come even to forget that we are hiding, and think that our assumed pretty face is what we really look like.

The gospel is proclaimed to what we really are, whether we like it or not. God's call to us now is, as it was to Adam, to come out of hiding. There can be no question of our attracting his favour by any amount of spiritual make-up. His love is the ultimate source of our very existence; there is no antecedent beauty on our part. His love which called us out of non-existence calls to us still to come out of the unreality of our 'worldliness' into the daylight of his truth.

If people are not prepared to come to terms with the truth of what they are—either the truth of their total dependence on God or the truth of their actual, sinful and painful, condition—they are likely to be offended by a message which will have no truck with their defensive 'face'. And they are likely to react with hostility.

130

This is one reason why an authentic proclamation of God's peace may win persecution in return.

But even when, out of honesty or just sheer pain, people are prepared to come out of hiding, the way is likely to be long and difficult. We may well wish to respond to the invitation of God's love, which claims to be able to cope with the whole truth of what we are; but will we actually be able to trust it? If it is true that the human race has been building up for millennia a habit of suspicion, as seems to be the case, we cannot expect it to be an easy process to disburden ourselves of it.

And where suspicion is trying to learn trust, it is likely to trust only in a tentative, exploratory way at first. And it will probe the claim that love is unconditional by putting it to the test. This is why people who are just beginning to accept that they are loved, genuinely and for their own sake, not for the faces they hide behind, often react to love by, almost deliberately, making themselves awkward. It is as if they were throwing down a challenge: 'You say you love me for what I really am. All right, then, see if you can love *this*.' The ingrained habit of suspicion can test love only by hurting it. And deep distrust may have to inflict deep hurt before it can rest content.

And it is not only for the sake of the other that our profession of love must be tested. After all, God tests those who claim to love him, and yet he does not need to conduct experiments to discover what his creatures are like. God tested Abraham, God tested his people in the desert; God tested his Son, for our sake, before his public mission began. And in him we too are tested, and it is for our sake.[12] This testing confronts us with our own reality, and it is this reality which we must surrender to God for our redemption.

It would probably be true to say that for most of us, if not all, both processes are in fact going on at once. We are having our own hearts searched out to see what love is really there, and we are also probing love to see whether we are prepared to trust it. And it is what we find from the first process that we must entrust to the love which we are assured of by the second process.

And presiding over the whole operation, there stands the cross of Christ. There we see man tested to the very limit and not wavering in love or infidelity. On the cross of Christ the testing of God's people finally discloses a human response that is wholly true. And it is broken open so that we may share it. Here we find the unflinching faith and hope and love, which must become our very lifeblood, but of which, left to ourselves, we could never begin to be capable.

But here also is the ultimate test of God's love. In Christ, God provokes man to do his very worst; and he continues to love. Here, then, is a love which has demonstrated that it does not flinch even when we do our worst. It is a love which can absorb our pathological drive to probe and wound. 'He has borne our diseases' (Matt. 8:17); and that means both that he has carried them away and disposed of them, and that he has endured them, loving 'to the end' (John 13:1).

The cross of Christ confronts us both with God's supreme consolation—'Whatever you are, I can love you'—and with his supreme insult—'This is what you do to love, this is what you are really like.' In accepting God's love for ourselves, we must also accept the judgement of that insult. Love, in our broken world of sin, can never be other than forgiveness.

And those who are prepared to accept, or at least to try to accept, that all-forgiving love, are at once caught up in the prophetic task of declaring it to the world. And that will always mean declaring both the insult and the comfort. And it cannot be declared as a matter of mere information. Those who speak the word of God's love are drawn into it themselves, and become vehicles for it. The Holy Spirit, the Spirit of prophecy, who makes us able to speak, makes us also able to love with the same love which is shown forth on the cross. And it will in turn provoke people to probe it. And, though we may not all be persecuted to the point of death as a result of this, we must all be prepared to be wounded, and wounded precisely because we have become carriers of God's love.

It is surely no accident that the people who do get martyred are often precisely the people who have shown most love. We are sometimes bewildered when we hear, for instance, of devoted missionaries being killed by those whom they have served for years with unfailing generosity. 'Why them?' we ask in perplexity and distress. Could it not be that it is precisely their devoted service which draws martyrdom towards them? Because they have been seen to love, they give confidence to those who are unsure of love; but this confidence eventually becomes a need to probe further. The final sacrifice is very much a sacrifice of love, and who can say what its fruit may be?

In some of the saints we read about a yearning for martyrdom and suffering that makes most of us decidedly uncomfortable. But maybe here we can at least glimpse something of that logic which leads from love to suffering. There is a sense in which love must be prepared to express itself in suffering. To love, and to love to the very end, in this sick world of ours, is to give oneself as a kind of sacrifice. And it would be foolhardly to deny the evidence of the saints that even now there is a kind of blessedness attached to being such a sacrifice for love.

Of course, we must not romanticize martyrdom. Sometimes perhaps we think grandly to ourselves of the great sacrifices we are going to make and daydream of heroic feats we shall perform for the Lord. We can almost hear the applause in heaven and on earth as we climb to our martyrdom.

But that is not what it is like at all. For most of us, being persecuted for the sake of Christ is not going to mean anything very public and glorious; it is going to mean an endless and boring array of petty harassments. And the 'they' who persecute us will, in all probability, not be obvious enemies, but our friends and neighbours, and, not least, ourselves.

The coming of God's love into our world is a highly explosive occurrence, and the acceptance of it in the church is not a simple matter which we can expect to take in our stride. The church is the workshop in which the new humanity is forged, and the process involves a lot of banging and puffing and burning and cutting. We and all those who surround us will be caught up in many strange adventures before the tale is done. And in these adventures we hurt ourselves and each other. That is how most of us will be persecuted by 'them'. The old Adam in ourselves and in our companions is quite sufficient to provide us with the hostility and aggression required to bring us within the scope of this last beatitude.

It is in the everyday hurly-burly of life that most of us, most of the time, must seek the application of the beatitude of the persecuted. We must try to see the hurts and insults that we administer to and receive from ourselves and one another as being all part of the process whereby God's peace and love are declared into the world of sin, so that redemption can take place. And so we can know that already a certain blessedness enfolds them.

And it is not wholly unreasonable to expect that we may, sometimes, even find ourselves beginning to jump for joy. This process of declaring and making present God's peace and love into our world is the way in which we are brought more deeply into the truth of what we are as God's creatures and so, however much pain it causes, it will also inevitably bring us ever closer to the source of genuine vitality within us. If we jump for joy, it is because, in spite of everything, we discover the fountain of life bubbling up within us. The truth will set us free, as our Lord said; the truth of what we are will set us free from our stiffness and our grim propriety. And even if it takes a bit of persecution to get us to the point of truth, we shall still surely find an urge within us to give vent to our freedom and our sense of being alive. This is, of course, not a matter of conforming ourselves to any prescribed pattern of enthusiastic self-expression, such as a variety of modern movements, both sacred and profane, are eager to inculcate. It is a matter of complete spontaneity, unprogrammed and unpredictable in its expression and in its occurrences. And it is more likely to make us feel foolish, if we happen to become self-conscious about it, than to make us feel that at last we have attained to any kind of spiritual prowess.

But if this is to be more than just a quirk of human psychology, we must not forget that the life which wells up in us spontaneously is at the same time the life which pours out from the broken heart of Christ. There is no Holy Spirit for us unless the Son of God is lifted up in sacrifice upon the cross (John 7:39). And so our jumping for joy brings us back to that figure in whom all the beatitudes come together into their final synthesis.

It is in the light of Calvary that we can see what it means for us to confess our poverty and our helplessness and to renounce the attempt to overcome them on our own. It is there that we accept our suffering and turn it into a compassion with all the pains that men bear, bundled together as they are in the suffering of Christ. It is there that we discover and fortify our charitable yearning for all righteousness to be revealed, while at the same time tempering it with a deep and comprehensive mercy, which we know we need ourselves and which we hope to share with all men. And so we come imperceptibly to see everything more purely in the light of

134

God's seeing of all that he has made, and so we come to be able at least to whisper the truth of the infinite peace of God's will even in the midst of the storms and contentions of life in this world. *Stat crux dum volvitur orbis.* It is the cross and only the cross that provides a constant point of reference in the chaos of our world, because there is all our poverty and helplessness and pain, all our yearning and all our mutual injustice, taken up into the stillness of God's everlasting love and made into the instrument and revelation of his unchanging will. So in all of it, beatitude is formed in the depth of our individual and churchly lives, giving us at least a courage to persevere until all joy is revealed. And so our hope comes to be focused on God's rule rather than our own, and it comes also to expand, reaching far beyond the wildest dreams of earthly planners, because it homes in on that fullness of blessing which God has in store for those who love him, which 'eye has not seen and ear has not heard and it has not entered the heart of man to conceive it' (1 Cor. 2:9).

General Abbreviations

General abbreviations, used in the Notes and Bibliography, are listed here; for abbreviations for particular works cited, see the Bibliography under relevant authors.

ACW	Ancient Christian Writers (London & Westminster, Maryland).
ANF	Ante-Nicene Fathers (currently available from Eerdmans, Grand Rapids, Michigan).
AP	*Apophthegmata Patrum* (=*Sayings of the Desert Fathers*). See the Bibliography for details.
BT	Babylonian Talmud. See the Bibliography for details.
Budé	Édition 'Les Belles Lettres', Paris.
CF	Cistercian Fathers (Kalamazoo).
CSCO	Corpus Scriptorum Christianorum Orientalium (Louvain).
CWS	Classics of Western Spirituality (London & New York).
DS	H. Denzinger, *Enchiridion Symbolorum*, revised by A. Schönmetzer.
ET	English translation.
EvT	A. Cohen, *Everyman's Talmud* (Everyman 1949).
FC	Fathers of the Church (New York, later Washington D.C.).
FT	French translation.
GCS	Griechischen Christlichen Schriftsteller (Leipzig, later Berlin).
GT	German translation.

LCL	Loeb Classical Library (Harvard & London).
LF	Library of the Fathers (Oxford).
LT	Latin translation.
MR	*Midrash Rabbah*. See the Bibliography for details.
NPNF	Nicene and Post-Nicene Fathers (currently available from Eerdmans, Grand Rapids, Michigan).
PG	Migne, *Patrologia Graeca*.
PL	Migne, *Patrologia Latina*.
PO	Graffin, *Patrologia Orientalis* (Paris).
PPJ	E. P. Sanders, *Paul and Palestinian Judaism* (London 1977).
PS	Graffin, *Patrologia Syriaca* (Paris).
SC	Sources Chrétiennes (Paris).
ST	St Thomas Aquinas, *Summa Theologiae*.
T	Text: this refers to critical editions of original texts.

Notes

Introduction

[1] Ephrem, *Commentary on the Diatessaron*, I 19.

Chapter One

[1] Bossuet, *Méd. Év.*, I 1 (p. 65).
[2] *Nine Ways*, 7 (T p. 102; ET p. 38).
[3] *SDM* I 11, II 38.
[4] Cf. O. Lottin, *Psychologie et morale aux XIIe et XIIIe siècles*, III (Louvain 1949), pp. 360, 376, 389, 404, etc.
[5] Cf. H. L. Strack & P. Billerbeck, *Kommentar zum Neuen Testament aus Talmud und Midrasch*, II (Munich 1924), on Luke 18:11. Our evidence for the Pharisees is deplorably scant, but there seems no reason to suppose that later Jewish texts expressing a strong view of dependence on God for all human goodness, including moral goodness, do not represent the attitude of the Pharisees. Josephus, at least, appears to regard it as a difference between them and the Sadducees that the latter ascribe moral achievement simply to human free will, whereas the Pharisees regard it as deriving from God (*Bell Jud*, II 8, 14). Cf. Emil Schürer, *The History of the Jewish People in the Age of Jesus Christ*, revised ed. by Geza Vermes, Fergus Millar & Matthew Black, vol. ii (Edinburgh, 1979) pp. 392ff; E. P. Sanders, *Paul and Palestinian Judaism* (London 1977), pp. 224, 297. The most impressive relevant Rabbinic texts are in BT *Ber* 16b–17a. One element in the picture is the doctrine that the soul implanted in each one of us by God is aboriginally completely pure: BT *Nid* 30b; *Shab* 152b; MR Lev 18:1; Philo, *Quis rerum* 105ff. Cf. Hermas 28 (= *Mand* III), 109 (= *Sim* IX 32). That the nature of man is essentially good, in spite of sin, is an important element in Greek Christian

theology of grace: cf. Athanasius, *VA* 20 (PG 26:872–3); Gregory of Nyssa, *Virg* XII 2–3 (= J 297.24–302.4). Pelagius tried to express the same thought, *Dem* 2 (PL 30:16–17), but fell foul of Augustine, which is why the idea does not generally feature in later western thought on the subject. For the doctrine that God reinforces every good move we make: BT *Shab* 104a, *Yom* 39a. Many relevant texts can be found in *Forms of Prayer for Jewish Worship*, I pp. 212ff (published by The Reform Synagogues of Great Britain 1977).

[6] Graham Greene, *The Power and the Glory*, III ch. 1, p. 173.

[7] *In Sent* I d.1 q.2, p. 14.

[8] Eckhart, QMa V 116–7 (= QMi 146–7, C1Fab 156, C1Fon 153); Suso *Little Book of Truth*, V (T p. 346, ET p. 195).

[9] Cf. Boethius, *Consolation of Philosophy*, V prose 6.

[10] Mary Westmacott (= Agatha Christie), *Absent in the Spring*, ch. 5, p. 70.

[11] *VM* I 5 (= J 3:12–14).

[12] *VM* II 163–9 (= J 87–9).

[13] *Cant* V (= J 158–60, PG 44:876).

[14] Cf. Thérèse of Lisieux, *DE* 6.8.8. (T pp. 308–9, ET p. 89): in response to her sister's question what she understood by 'remaining a little child before the good God', she said,

It is recognizing one's nothingness (*son néant*), expecting everything from the good God, just as a little child expects everything from its father; it is not getting anxious about anything, not trying to make one's fortune. Even with the poor, a child is always given what it needs; but as soon as it grows up, its father refuses to go on supporting it and says to it: 'Now you must go and work, you can look after yourself.' It is to avoid having that said to me that I have always refused to grow up, because I felt that I was quite incapable of earning my living (*gagner ma vie*), earning my eternal life in heaven. So I have remained always little, having nothing else to do except pick flowers, flowers of love and sacrifice, and to offer them to the good God to give him pleasure. Being little is also not attributing to oneself the virtues that one practises, as if one believed oneself capable of achieving something, but recognizing that the good God puts this treasure into the hands of his little child for it to make use of it whenever it needs to; but it is always the good God's treasure. Finally it is never being disheartened by one's faults, because children often fall, but they are too little to do themselves much harm.

[15] *Ab* p. 34 (ET II 2 §4).

[16] Cf. *Cloud of Unknowing*, ch. 68.

[17] Eckhart, QMa V 203–4 (= QMi 59–60, C1Fab 68–9, C1Fon 65); QMa II 473–4 (= QMi 265, PE I 259).

[18] QMa I 91 (= QMi 180, W 117).

[19] QMa V 23 (= QMi 111, C1Fab 119, C1Fon 116).

[20] QMa III 16 (= QMi 367, PE I 120).
[21] QMa V 206 (=QMi 61, ClFab 70, ClFon 66); QMa II 81–2 (=QMi 292, W 137).
[22] *AP* Nau 11.

Chapter Two

[1] Barnabas, 6:13.

[2] Clement of Alexandria, *QDS* 40:1, suggests the contrary; but St Thomas, *ST* Ia q.25 a.4, is surely correct in saying that there is a contradiction involved in the suggestion that what has happened can be made not to have happened.

[3] Charles Williams, *He Came down from Heaven*, ch. 2–4.

[4] MR Gen 9:7.

[5] Mishnah, *Ber* 9:5.

[6] Barnabas, 4:10.

[7] Ibid., 15:6–7.

[8] Ibid., 6:18.

[9] Ibid., 4:13.

[10] Cf. *Conf* IV 18–19, V 2, X 16.

[11] Vincent Ferrer, *Vit Spir* V (ET pp. 66f).

[12] *DE* 29.7.3 (T p. 286, ET p. 69).

Chapter Three

[1] Nathan, 28 (p. 117).

[2] BT *Ber* 5b. Cf. *EvT*, p. 365.

[3] BT *Taan* 25a. For other stories, see MR Exod 52:3.

[4] Texts conveniently assembled in *EvT*, pp.364ff.

[5] E.g. Barnabas, 18:2; Ignatius, *Eph* 17:1, 19:1, *Magn* 1:2; *Acts of Judas Thomas*, 32; *Ascension of Isaiah*, 4:2.

[6] Hermas 50:1–5 (= *Sim* I).

[7] Hermas 74:2 (= *Sim* VIII 8), 75 (= *Sim* VIII 9), 96:3 (= *Sim* IX 19), 97:2 (= *Sim* IX 20), 103:5 (= *Sim* IX 26). For the Jewish background to the view that the essential and fatal sin is always that of denying the covenant, see Sanders, *PPJ*, pp. 92–6, 134–6.

[8] Gospel of Thomas, logion 21.

[9] On the social and economic position of Christians in the first few centuries, see R. M. Grant, *Early Christianity and Society* (London 1978).

[10] Hermas 51 (= *Sim* II), 97 (= *Sim* IX 20). This is a Jewish doctrine: cf BT *BB* 10a.

[11] Heraclitus, B 91 (DK) (= 40(c3) M).

[12] Plato, *Cratylus* 439 Cff.

[13] Robert Herrick, *To the Virgins, to make much of Time*, 1.

[14] Andrew Marvell, *To his coy Mistress*, 22.

[15] Traherne, *Centuries* I 34.

[16] Ibid., II 77.

[17] Eckhart, QMa I 77 (= QMi 174, C1Nel 233, W 109).

[18] Cf. G. L. Prestige, *God in Patristic Thought* (London 1952), pp. 291ff.

[19] MR Gen 8:9, 17:2; BT *Yeb* 63a.

[20] Basil, *RF* 3:1 (PG 31:917A).

[21] Cf. J. Pieper, *Ueber die Hoffnung* (Munich 1949), pp. 28–30.

[22] G. K. Chesterton, *The Innocence of Father Brown (The Three Tools of Death)*, p. 246.

[23] Cf. C. S. Lewis, *Screwtape Letters* XVII.

[24] Eckhart, QMa II 502 (= QMi 308, PE I 220).

[25] QMi 273 (= C1Nel 184), QMa II 31 (= QMi 385, W 99–100).

[26] QMa I 196–7 (= QMi 214–5, C1Nel 225).

Chapter Four

[1] Cf. 4 Esdras 3:20ff, 7:116ff.

[2] Cf. R. Mach, *Der Zaddik in Talmud und Midrasch* (Leiden 1957), ch. 7–8; G. Vermes, *Scripture and Tradition in Judaism* (2nd edition, Leiden, 1973), pp. 206ff; E. P. Sanders, *PPJ*, pp. 183ff. For a Rabbinic discussion of the duration of the effect of the merits of the fathers, see MR Lev 36:5–6.

[3] On the *zaddiq* in Judaism, see R. Mach, op. cit.; S. H. Dresner, *The Zaddik* (New York 1974).

[4] Diognetus, 6:1. For the *zaddiq* in Christianity, see Simon Tugwell, *New Heaven? New Earth?* (London 1976), p. 155 n.11 with further references. The most important text in Clement of Alexandria is *QDS* 36. Cf. also Gospel of Thomas, logion 12 (Jewish analogues to which are cited in J. É. Ménard, *L'Évangile selon Thomas* (Leiden 1975), p. 97.

[5] Acts 3:14, 7:52. Cf. Richard N. Longenecker, *The Christology of Early Jewish Christianity* (London 1970), pp. 46f.

[6] Ionesco, *Un homme en question*, p. 133.

[7] Cf. *ST* Ia q.19 a.1 ad 1.

[8] Eckhart, QMa V 43 (= QMi 125, C1Fab 133, C1Fon 130), QMa II 59 (= QMi 299, W 141), QMi 371 (=PE II 118).

[9] Angelus Silesius, *Cherubinischer Wandersmann* I 289.

[10] Emily Dickinson *Poems* 1255 (Longing is like the seed).

[11] *Screwtape Letters* XIII, pp. 66–9.

[12] E.g. Eckhart, QMa V 282 (= QMi 90–1, ClFab 98, ClFon 95), QMa I 90 (= QMi 180, W 117), QMa I 113 (= QMi 186, ClNel 189), QMa II 253–5 (= QMi 267, ClFab 53, ClFon 49), QMa II 26–7 (= QMi 383–4, W 98).

[13] QMa I 91–2 (=QMi 180, W 118).

[14] *ST* Ia IIae q.3 a.1, q.8 a.1, q.9 a.6, q.10 a.1.

[15] *ST* Ia IIae q.1.a.1.

[16] Eckhart, QMa I 91 (=QMi 180, W 117).

[17]*Didache*, 10:6.

[18] Cf. Bl. Jordan's reassurance to his travelling companions, when they found that they had strayed from their path, 'Never mind, it is all part of the way to heaven' (*Lives of the Brethren*, T p. 106, ET IV vi).

[19] Cf. St Thomas, *ST* Ia q.22 a.2 & 3; *de Pot* q.3 a.5 & 7.

[20] E.g. de Caussade, *Lettres* I, p. 268 (ET 1934 pp. 13f): 'I wish I could shout out everywhere, "Self-abandonment! Self-abandonment!" And what then? Again, self-abandonment, but self-abandonment without limits and without reserve.' Cf. Julian of Norwich, ch. 10, 11, 52 & 61. Thérèse of Lisieux, *Hist* IX, pp. 214–5; *DE* 15.6.1 (T p. 229, ET p. 21); *DE* 15.6.1 (T p. 229, ET p. 21).

[21] Cf. Aelred Squire, *Asking the Fathers* (London 1973), pp. 214–23.

[22] Cf. de Caussade, *Ab*, pp. 99–101 (ET I 2 §4); *Lettres* I, pp. 83–4 (ET 1936, pp. 83f).

[23] It is still well worth reading Father Faber's chapters on the easiness of salvation in Part III of *The Creator and the Creature*, ch. 1–2.

[24] Cf. Irenaeus, *a.H.* V 15, 2: *opera Dei plasmatio est hominis*.

[25] Julian, ch. 38 & 27. Sin is known only by the pain it causes, and this is essentially Christ's pain; if it is also ours, ours is in his, and that is what makes it significant (cf. ch. 18, and especially ch. 28).

[26] Hermas 9:6 (= *Vis* III 1).

[27] Julian, ch. 34, 45 & 82.

[28] *Bhagavad Gita*, 5:11–12.

[29] *DE* 15.5.5. (T p. 208, ET p. 4).

Chapter Five

[1] Ignatius, *Rom* 3:3.

[2] Light is shed on Ignatius' paradox by Hermes Trismegistos, V, sub-titled, 'That God, being unmanifest, is the most manifest of all'. The point in this tractate is that all manifest being is limited to its own particular

sphere of manifestation, but God, who is hidden in himself, is manifested in everything, and so is far more manifest than any particular manifest thing. Similarly for Ignatius the ascended (disappeared) Lord is far more universally present in his power than he was when his presence was localized in the incarnation.

[3] Origen, *Or* 20:2.

[4] E.g. Euripides, *Troades* 884ff, quoted by Proclus, *Plat Theol* I 15, and possibly referred to by Cyril of Alexandria, *Quod Chr Unus* 760C (ET p. 296); Numenius, fragment 2, quoted by Eusebius, *PE* XI 22:1.

[5] Cf. Gospel of Truth, 29. It is tempting to say that it is characteristic of *hysterêma* to produce hysterical behaviour, and, if Paula Fredriksen is right (*Hysteria and the Gnostic Myths of Creation*, Vigiliae Christianae 33 (1979) pp. 287–90, the pun would be an ancient one: *hysterêma* was meant to suggest a connexion with *hystera* (womb), from which 'hysteria' is derived.

[6] Origen, *Cels* II 67:21–2 (SC) (= GCS I p. 189:12–13). Origen several times refers to the curious belief that Christ's physical appearance varied, so that he appeared quite differently to different people and at different times (*Comm in Matt* XII 36; *Ser in Matt* 100). Ephrem appears to be referring to the same belief in *HFid* 31:11 (ET p. 207). It appears in an extreme form in Acts of John, 88–93. Presumably it is related in some way to the curious hints in the biblical resurrection stories that the risen Lord is somehow not straightforwardly recognizable. People have to *discover* that it is indeed the Lord. The theological sense of this is surely that even Christ, even the risen Christ, cannot make God (or his own divine nature) *visible* to us in quite the same way that tables and chairs are visible. His full identity can be disclosed only in a variety of appearances.

There is also a problem about the way in which God (or Christ's divine nature) can be said to be fully and personally present in the human person of Christ. In him 'all the fullness of the Godhead dwells' (Col. 2:9); but this cannot mean that somehow the body of Christ *contains* the whole of Godhead. God is not exhausted in the physical presence of Christ. If God is in Christ is a uniquely intense way, this still cannot mean that he is consequently absent from everywhere else. It was a sound theological instinct that made St Thomas adapt the Advent hymn in the way that he did for his Corpus Christi office. Where the Advent hymn said (in the older version found, for instance, in the old Dominican breviary):

Verbum supernum prodiens
A Patre olim exiens,

St Thomas wrote:

Verbum supernum prodiens,
Nec Patris linquens dexteram.

143

In spite of the incarnation, the hiddenness and the universal presence of the Son of God remain. Similarly the Real Presence of Christ in the eucharistic elements does not mean that he is less present elsewhere, nor does the multiplication of consecrated hosts mean that he is somehow bilocating. Christ's presence in the host is not *local*, as if he were present in it in the same way that a banana occupies its own particular place (cf. *ST* IIIa q.76 a.5). Even the most privileged modes of divine self-giving and self-disclosure must never be regarded as *confining* God.

[7] Cf. Simon Tugwell, *The Incomprehensibility of God* (New Blackfriars November 1979).

[8] Aeschylus, *Agamemnon* 211, 218.

[9] Cf. Rollo May, *LW* pp. 14ff, 184; *PI* pp. 21ff.

[10] Cf. Irenaeus, *a.H.* V 35–6.

[11] Ephrem, *Commentary on Genesis* II 10.

[12] Cf. Simon Tugwell, 'The Speech-Giving IIRIT', IN *New Heaven? New Earth?* (London 1976).

[13] Cf. Rollo May, *LW* pp. 23–4, 127–8; *PI* pp. 48–50, 233 ('Art is a substitute for violence').

Chapter Six

[1] E.g. Barnabas, 6:17–19; *Sibylline Oracles*, VIII 256–68; Origen, *Princ* III 6:1; Methodius, *Symp* I iv 23; Tertullian, *Res* 6:3ff; Irenaeus, *Dem* 32, 97.

[2] Cf. Gospel of Truth, 17:10ff.

[3] It is a commonplace of patristic theology that man was cast out of Paradise into 'this world'. e.g. Irenaeus, *a.H.* V 5:1; Origen, *Josh* VI 4. See Antonio Orbe, *Antropología de S. Ireneo* (Madrid 1969), p. 198 n. 21.

[4] Cf. *ST* Ia q.87 a.1.

[5] *ST* Ia IIae q.110 a.4.

[6] Cf. Ignatius, *Eph* 15:1–2; Ephrem, *HFid* 11:5–9 (ET pp. 149–50).

[7] Cf. Irenaeus, *a.H.* IV 6:6 (SC and ET) (= IV 11:4 Harvey).

[8] George Macdonald, *Lilith*, ch. 43, p. 255.

[9] Cf. Jean Leclercq, *La Liturgie et les paradoxes Chrétiens* (Paris 1963), ch. 7.

[10] Cf. C. S. Lewis, *Pilgrim's Regress* IV ch. 3, pp. 91–2.

[11] Augustine, *Conf* VII 16.

[12] Vatican II, *Sacrosanctum Concilium* (Constitution on the Liturgy), 10.

Chapter Seven

[1] Cf. Rollo May, *LW* pp. 27–8, 59.

[2] It is interesting that the author of the Anglo-Saxon *Advent Lyrics* uses imagery suggesting a conflation of Christ's descent to earth with his descent into Hell (*Advent Lyrics* V 12–15 (= *Christ* 115–18); cf. *Guthlac* 677–80 (about Hell). Life on this earth, as it stands, is simply disguised death and provisional damnation.

[3] Gregory of Nyssa, *VM* II 3 (= J 34:11); cf. *Eccl* VI (=J 380: 3, PG 44:701D). The reference to Aristotle, *Eth Nic* IV 7, in the 2nd edition of SC1, p. 33, repeated by Malherbe and Fergusson, p. 157, is both inaccurate and irrelevant. The reference should be to III 7 (1113b18), and it is corrected in the 3rd edition of SC 1. But it is still nothing to do with the matter in hand. More pertinent is Clement of Alexandria, *Str* VII 13:3, which states that the gnostic creates himself.

[4] *SDM* I 11. Cf. St Thomas, *in Matt* 424. It is interesting to compare the role of awareness of *dukkha* in Buddhism. Cf. E. Conze, *Buddhism* (New York 1959, pp. 45ff). Cf. *Dhammapada* 190–2: 'He who seeks refuge in the Buddha, the Dhamma, and the Sangha, he who sees with right knowledge the Four Noble Truths—Sorrow (*Dukkha*), the Cause of Sorrow, the Transcending of Sorrow, and the Noble Eightfold Path which leads to the Cessation of Sorrow—This indeed is refuge secure; this indeed is refuge supreme. Seeking such refuge one is released from all sorrow.'

[5] Benedict Green, C.R. draws my attention to Matt. 9:15 where 'mourning' corresponds to the penitential 'fasting' in Mark 2:19.

[6] 4 Esdras 7:116f. The translation, 'It would have been better not to have given the earth to Adam' is also possible, and seems to be favoured by Bensly, judging from his note in the Index, under *Adam*; but the rendering given in my text is supported by the other versions, and is the one favoured by Charles.

[7] Cf. Eckhart, QMa III 490 (= QMi 287, W 86–7); de Caussade, *Ab* p. 136 (no ET).

[8] E.g. de Caussade, *Lettres* I, pp. 65–6 (ET 1934 p. 19), p. 90 (ET 1936 p. 80), p. 280 (ET 1936 p. 47); Thérèse of Lisieux, *CG* I, p. 459 (ET p. 80).

[9] *Hist* X, p. 243.

[10] *Mors nostra est eius morte redempta* (Missale Romanum, *Praefatio Paschalis* II). It is unfortunate that the English versions of this important text have seriously altered the sense.

[11] Charles Williams, *Taliessin through Logres* (Oxford, pp. 81f; Grand Rapids, pp. 99f).

[12] C. S. Lewis, *Williams and the Arthuriad*, p.359.

[13] Emily Dickinson, *Poems* 652 ('A Prison gets to be a friend').

[14] Heinrich Heine, 'Ich unglücksel'ger Atlas'. The translation was first

published in the *Pelican Record* 34 (1963), p. 121. I am grateful to Sir Kenneth Dover, the President of Corpus Christi College, for permission to reprint it here.

Chapter Eight

[1] C.S. Lewis, *Voyage to Venus*, ch. 3, pp. 36f.

[2] Thomas Cantipratanus, *de Apibus* II x 10; Acts of Dominican General Chapter, 1240.

[3] Evagrius, *Prakt* 7.

[4] *VM* II 105 (= J 65:3–4).

[5] *VM* II 142 (= J 78:20–22).

[6] Evagrius, *Prakt* 16.

[7] *AP* Paphnutius 5.

[8] Cf. Teles, II, with Hense's note to p.7 lines 8ff. Bernard, *Ep* 1:11–12.

[9] *ST* Ia q.12 a.1.

[10] Augustine, *Trin* XIII 5:8. Cf. *ST* Ia IIae q.3 a.4.

[11] Basil, *Ep* 151. Cf. Epictetus I 12:15, II 14:7, *Enchiridion* 8; Seneca, *Ep* 54:7.

[12] Barnabas, 15:7.

[13] Boccaccio, *Il Filostrato* VIII 27ff.

[14] Chaucer, *Troilus* V 1808–13.

[15] Ibid., V 1748–50.

[16] Ibid., V 1814–22.

[17] Ibid., V 1835–48. C. S. Lewis refers to this passage in a letter to Arthur Greeves in connexion with his (Lewis') conversion to belief in God, 'That is another of the beauties of coming, I won't say, to religion but to an attempt at religion—one finds oneself on the main road with all humanity, and can compare notes with an endless succession of previous travellers. It is emphatically coming home: as Chaucer says "Returneth *home* from worldly vanitee" ' (Letter 130, pp. 333–4). Lewis also draws attention to the same phrase in *The Allegory of Love*, ch. 4 (ii), p. 179.

[18] *Cloud of Unknowing*, ch. 42. Modern translators are generally rather coy in their rendering of *rechelesnes;* but it is important to be aware that, for this author as for ourselves, it is a word with generally *bad* connotations: cf. EETS 218, p. 38:7–8, EETS 231, pp. 49:18, 50:18–19, 55:3, 89:3. Father Baker entirely falsifies the picture by taking it to mean 'recklessness *about*' these things, 'that is, by not loving them or affecting them' (p. 387).

[19] E.g. Bernard, *Cant* 74:3; William of St Thierry, *Cant* 33. The doctrine comes from Augustine and Gregory; e.g. Augustine, *Enarr. in Ps 83*, 3; *in Ps 87*, 14; Gregory, *Moral V* 6, XXVI 34; *Hom. in Ev.* II 25:2.

[20] *ST* Ia q.12 a.6.

[21] Guigo II, *Scala* 10.

[22] Basil, *Hex* VI 1 (120A), *Spir* 36.

[23] QMa V 278–9 (=QMi 89, ClFab 96–7, ClFon 93).

[24] St Thomas, *CG* III 69.

[25] *Div Nom* IV 13 (PG 3:712AB).

[26] Cf. Guigo II, *Scala* 8.

Chapter Nine

[1] Cf. Evagrius, *Prakt* 63, *KG* IV 47.

[2] When St Catherine of Siena took to herself responsibility for all the ills of the world, she meant something very precise: if she had lived up to the immense graces God had given her, she would have had a universal effect for good throughout the world, since perfect charity is the most powerful force for good that exists in creation. Her failure to be as charitable as she could have been is therefore responsible for the lack of blessing that should have been. See Raymund of Capua, *Life*, 1st Prologue, 13 (A.SS. 12:865D). Cf. Catherine, *Dial* II (T p. 4). Cf. Simon Tugwell, *The Way of the Preacher* (London 1979), pp. 48–50.

[3] E.g. Origen, *Cels* IV 40; Ambrose, *Apol Dav 2*, 71; Aelred, *Serm Inediti*, p. 54:7–8; Missale Gallicanum Vetus, p. 78 quoted in ET in George Every, *Christian Mythology* (London 1970), p. 28; Julian, ch. 51.

[4] Cf. M. Buber, *Tales of the Hasidim: The Early Masters* (New York 1947), p. 251: 'Before his death, Rabbi Zusya said, "In the coming world, they will not ask me, 'Why were you not Moses?' They will ask me, 'Why were you not Zusya?' " '.)

[5] Cf. St Thomas, *Quodl* IV a.6.

[6] Cf. C. S. Lewis, *The Great Divorce*, pp. 110ff.

[7] Cf. the tradition found in Augustine, *CD* XXII 1, that the human beings who are saved replace the fallen angels, 'so that the heavenly city should not be deprived of its proper number of citizens'.

[8] In Acts 3:21 the final end of this world is referred to as 'the time of the *apokatastasis*, the restoration, of everything'. But the word came to be associated particularly with the doctrine of universal salvation, including the eventual salvation of the devil. This was taught by Origen (texts assembled in J. Quasten, *Patrology* II. Utrecht & Westminster, Ma. 1953, pp. 87–90), and was condemned by a Council in Constantinople in 543 (DS 411).

[9] Julian, ch. 34, cf. ch. 11.

[10] Julian, ch. 32–3.

[11] Cf. Evagrius, *Prakt* 24.

[12] Cf. Cassian, *Inst* VIII 7–9; Gregory, *Mor* V 83 (PL 75: 727B).

[13] *Didache*, 10:6.

[14] For the Christian tradition, cf. *Didache*, 4:6; Barnabas, 19:10–11; 2 Clement, 16:4; Chrysostom, *Cat* VII 27. For Judaism, cf *EvT*, p. 220 (citing BT *BB* 10a, *Ber* 55a).

[15] Cf. Clement of Alexandria, *QDS* 33:2.

[16] *ST* Ia q.23 a.5. This traditional Thomist thesis has not been universally accepted. Apart from the Jesuit Molinists, see Sanders, *PPJ* p. 92 (quoting *Sifre Deut.* 311); Hermas 72:2 (=*Sim* VIII 6); Clement of Alexandria, *Str* VII 107:5; Origen, *Phil* 25:2. But once the question has been formally raised, it is difficult to see how we could refuse the answer given by St Thomas, unless we are prepared to allow God's actions to be caused by acts of his own creatures, which is, on the face of it, nonsensical. *Scientia media* really does not resolve this difficulty.

[17] Clement of Alexandria, *QDS* 31:9. Cf. *Liber Graduum*, XXIV 7 (PS 3:725–8).

Chapter Ten

[1] *ST* IIa IIae q. 155 a.1.

[2] Cf. St Thomas, *in Matt* 849. Cf. Origen, *Mart* 32 (GCS p. 28:1–3).

[3] Cf. Irenaeus, *a.H.* V 9:1: 'Perfect man consists of flesh, soul and Spirit.' The context makes it clear that it is God's Spirit who is in question here. It is part of man's identity to have God's Spirit.

[4] Raymund of Capua, *Life* 179. Cf. also 90: One day Raymund visited Catherine when she was sick, and he saw her face changed and realized that he was looking into the face of Christ himself.

[5] On the doctrine of *anatta*, there is a useful pamphlet by Nyanaponika Thera, *Anatta and Nibbana* (Kandy 1959).

[6] *ST* Ia IIae Prologue.

[7] *Conf* III 11.

[8] *ST* Ia q.87 a.1.

[9] E.g. Philo, *Leg. All.* I 91; Gamaliel, cited in *Midrash on Psalms*, II, pp. 158–9; MR Lev 4:8; BT *Ber* 10a. Basil, *Ep* 235:2; Macarius, III 18:1. Cf. Cornelius Ernst, *Multiple Echo* (London 1979), pp. 225–38, *The Vocation of Nature*, with its conclusion, 'We cannot precisely delineate . . . how we are limited.'

[10] *Aut* I 2, cf. I 5.

[11] QMa I 11–12 (= QMi 155, ClNel 129, W 57–8).

[12] Cf. *ST* Ia q.14 a.5.

[13] Cf. Athanasius, *CG* 2:9.

[14] The interpretation of *apatheia* as purity of heart goes back to Cassian, cf. Owen Chadwick, *John Cassian*, 1st ed. (Cambridge 1960), p. 91, 2nd ed. (Cambridge 1968), p. 102.

[15] Evagrius, *Prakt* 1, *Or* 51 (52), *Ep 8*, 4.

[16] *Cant*, Prol (GCS pp. 75–8, ACW pp. 39–44, CWS pp. 231–4). The order of events in Gregory Thaumaturgus, *Orig* 93ff, is different: logic, physics, ethics, theology. The ingredients are the standard ones in most ancient schools of philosophy; their proper order was a matter of considerable controversy. The order: logic, ethics, physics, theology, corresponds to that of Chrysippus (*SVF* II 42), and to that which Sextus ascribes generally to 'the Stoics' (*adv. Math* VII 22), but clearly not all the Stoics were in agreement (cf. Posidonius, fragment 91). Philo, twice at least, follows the order: logic, ethics, physics (*Leg All* I 57, *Spec Leg* I 336), but once he prefers: physics, ethics, logic (*Agr* 14–15)—but this does not exclude the paedagogical order: logic, ethics, physics. Clement of Alexandria evidently thinks that the Paedagogos gives a preliminary course in practical ethics before delivering the pupil to the Didaskalos, but the Didaskalos also gives ethical teaching (cf. A. Méhat, *Étude sur les stromates*, (Paris 1966), p. 50). In fact there is a reciprocal relationship between ethics and physics: ethics ultimately derives from physics, in that our view of what kind of creature man is determines our view of what he should do (cf. Origen, *Comm in Matt* XVII 7, GGS p. 603: 14f); but nevertheless, it is only those who are sorted out morally who can see the truth about things (cf. Origen, *Cels* VI 67:25 (SC) (= GCS II p. 137:24–5); Basil, *Hex* I 1 (4A), so a certain kind of practical ethics must be taught first (cf. Origen, *Cels* VIII 51–2), and at least in this sense ethics counts as elementary study (cf. Origen, *Num* XXVII 1, GCS p. 256:5–8).

[17] Gospel of Thomas, logion 5. J. E. Ménard, *L'Évangile selon Thomas* (Leiden 1975), p. 85. Clement of Alexandria, *Str* II 45:4.

[18] Cyril of Jerusalem, *Cat* 9:2. Cf. Basil, *Hex* V 2 (97BC), V 9 (116B).

[19] *Cant*, Prol (GCS p. 67:5–16, ACW pp. 29–30, CWS p. 223). Cf. Basil, *Hex* VI 1 (117BC).

[20] Basil, *Hex* I 6 (16C).

[21] Cf. Gregory Thaumaturgus, *Orig* 111.

[22] E. g. *Hex* I 11 (28B), V 8 (113A), VI 1 (120AB).

[23] E.g. *Hex* I 10 (25A).

[24] *Met* 982b11–21.

[25] *Eth Nic* 1125a2.

[26] *ST* Ia IIae q.32 a.8.

[27] J. Pieper, *The Silence of St Thomas: The Negative Element in the Philosophy of St Thomas* (Chicago 1965), pp. 53ff.

[28] *ST* Ia IIae q.31 a.5.

[29] *Ar.*, *Anim.* 15.

[30] Cf. Simon Tugwell, *The Way of the Preacher* (London 1979), p. 92.

[31] Cf. Charles Williams, *The Figure of Beatrice*, pp. 46–51; C. S. Lewis, *Williams and the Arthuriad*, p. 302.

[32] *AP* Poemen 97.

[33] Guigo I, *Meditations* 49; cf. 222.

[34] *Div Nom* IV 20 (PG 3:720BC). Cf. Origen, *Mart* 47 (GCS p. 43:2–4): 'He who made us put in us a desire for true religion and communion with himself, which retains certain traces of the divine purpose even in our sins.' Cf. also Baudelaire, *Les Paradis artificiels* I 1: 'Alas! Man's vices, however full of horror we may suppose them to be, contain the proof . . . of his taste for infinity; only it is a taste that often misses its way' (Pl p. 402, MR p. 568).

[35] Romanos, *Cant* 10 (MT & ET) (= 21 SC).

[36] *Hist* I, pp. 35–6.

[37] Cf. de Caussade, *Lettres* I, pp. 63f (ET 1934, p. 17), p. 94 (no ET), pp. 184–5 (ET 1934, pp. 97–9).

[38] Cf. *AP* Nau 316.

[39] Cf. St Thomas, *de Malo* q.1 a.3.

[40] Cf. *ST* Ia IIae q.79 a.2.

[41] QMa V 207 (= QMi 61, C1Fab 70, C1Fon 66f).

[42] Rollo May, *PI* pp. 48–50,

[43] E.g. Augustine, *Serm.* 104:3 (PL 38:617–18); Bernard, *Serm. Ass* 3; Guerric, *Sermon* 50:4.

[44] QMa III 481ff (= QMi 280ff, W 79ff).

[45] *AP* Anthony 5; cf. *AP* Evagrius 5. The reference in 'it says' is presumably to an agraphon found elsewhere, e.g. Tertullian, *Bapt* 20; *Didascalia*, p. 38; *Apostolic Constitutions* II 8:2.

[46] *AP* Joseph of Panephysis 3, Sarah 1.

[47] Rollo May, *PI*, p. 238.

[48] *DE* 29.7.3 (T p. 286, ET p. 69).

[49] Rollo May, *PI* p. 256.

[50] Cf. Ionesco, *Un Homme en question*, p. 15.

[51] Letter to Paterne Berrichon, quoted in Enid Starkie, *Arthur Rimbaud* (London 1961), p. 237.

[52] Starkie, op. cit., p. 444.

[53] Ibid., pp. 423ff.

[54] Rimbaud, *Letter to Paul Demeny* (15 May 1871).

[55] Starkie, op. cit., pp. 291ff.

[56] Baudelaire, *Le voyage*, VIII stanza 2. Cf. also *Hymne à la beauté*, 1–4, 21–8:

Viens-tu du ciel profond ou sors-tu de l'abîme,
O Beauté? Ton regard, infernal et divin,
Verse confusément le bienfait et le crime,
Et l'on peut pour cela te comparer au vin. . . .

Que tu viennes du ciel ou de l'enfer, qu'importe,
O Beauté! monstre énorme, effrayant, ingénu!
Si ton oeil, ton souris, ton pied, m'ouvrent la porte
D'un Infini que j'aime et n'ai jamais connu?

De Satan ou de Dieu, qu'importe? Ange ou Sirène,
Qu'importe, si tu rends,—fée aux yeux de velours,
Rythme, parfum, lueur, ô mon unique reine!—
L'univers moins hideux et les instants moins lourds?

It is difficult to know exactly how far Baudelaire was prepared to identify himself with all the sentiments expressed in *Les Fleurs du mal*. Elsewhere he makes a clear distinction between different ways of seeking something that transcends the dreariness of this world. In some *Notes on Realism* he wrote, 'Poetry is what is most real, it is what is only completely true *in another world*' (MR p. 448). In the dedicatory letter prefacing *Les Paradis artificiels* he writes: 'Good sense tells us that things of earth barely exist; true reality is to be found only in dreams (Pl p. 399, MR p. 567). He then distinguishes between dreams which, like poetry, present us with something genuinely new, and the illusory, diabolical travesty of novelty produced by drugs (I 3; Pl pp. 408–9, MR pp. 570–1). His moral is astringent:

> Every man who does not accept the conditions of life sells his soul. It is easy to grasp the connexion that exists between the satanic creations of the poets and living creatures who have dedicated themselves to drugs. Man wanted to be God, and soon, in virtue of an inexorable moral law, there he is, lower than his true nature (I 5; Pl p. 438, MR p. 583).

In *Mon Coeur mis à nu* he concludes:

> At every moment we are crushed by the idea and the perception of time. There are only two ways to escape this nightmare—to forget it: pleasure and work. Pleasure exploits us. Work strengthens us. Let us choose. . . . One can only forget time in making use of it. . . . All that is lacking, for us to be completely healed of everything, wretchedness, sickness and melancholy, is the *taste for work* (Pl p. 669, MR pp. 640–1).

[57] Rollo May, *PI* p. 233.
[58] Ibid., pp. 236–7.
[59] *AP* Poemen 141.
[60] Baudelaire, *Un voyage à Cythère*, stanza 15.
[61] Serapion, *Euch* 12:4.

151

[62] PL 177:747A.

[63] PL 176:1101CD.

[64] Peter Calo, *Vita* 3.

[65] William of Tocco, *Vita* 34.

[66] Cf. *ST* IIa IIae q.83 a.1 ad 2.

[67] *ST* Ia IIae q.113 a.10. Augustine, *Trin* XIV 11.

[68] Rollo May, *PI* p. 233.

[69] Cf. Baudelaire's projected Epilogue to *Les Fleurs du mal*:

Anges revêtus d'or, de pourpre et d'hyacinthe,
O vous, soyez témoins que j'ai fait mon devoir
Comme un parfait chimiste et comme une âme sainte.

Car j'ai de chaque chose extrait la quintessence,
*Tu m'as donné ta boue et j'en ai fait de l'or. (*Pl p. 192, MR p. 129).

[70] Cf. Cavafy, *Notes on Ruskin*, 48, 57.

[71] Translated by Peter Jay, *The Song of Songs* (London 1975), 17.

Chapter Eleven

[1] *AP* Nau 134.

[2] Cf. R. Murray, New Testament Studies 21 (1974), p. 65.

[3] Cf. Ignatius, *Magn* 7:2;

[4] For a very full account of the different senses of *in pace* in Christian inscriptions, see the article by H. Leclercq, 'Paix', in *Dictionnaire d'archéologie Chrétienne*.

[5] Cf. Julian, ch. 39, for the same point expressed differently: 'Peace and love is ever in us, being and working, but we be not ever in peace and love.'

[6] QMa I 118 (= QMi 188, ClNel 191).

[7] *Un Homme en question*, p. 42.

[8] *Cloud of Unknowing*, ch. 32.

[9] Vatican II, *Lumen Gentium* (Constitution on the Church), 9.

[10] I cannot resist quoting part of a highly unusual comment on the Athanasian Creed from Charles Williams, *The Greater Trumps*:

All the first part went on its usual way; (Nancy) knew nothing about musical setting of creeds, so she couldn't tell what to think of this one. The men and the boys of the choir exchanged metaphysical confidences; they dared each other, in a kind of rapture—which, she supposed, was the setting—to deny the Trinity or the Unity; they pointed out, almost mischievously, that though they were compelled to say one thing, yet they were forbidden to say something else exactly like it; they went into particulars about an entirely impossible relationship, and concluded with an explanation that something wasn't true which the wildest dream of any man but the compiler of the creed could hardly have begun to imagine. All this Nancy half-ignored. But the second part—and it was of course the setting—for one verse held her. It was of course the setting, the chance that sent one boy's voice sounding exquisitely through the church. But the words which conveyed that beauty sounded to her full of sudden significance. The mingled voices of men and boys were proclaiming the nature of Christ—'God and man is one in Christ'; then the boys fell silent, and the men went on, 'One, not by conversion of the Godhead into flesh, but by taking of the manhood into God'. On the assertion they ceased, and the boys rushed joyously in, 'One altogether, not'—they looked at the idea and tossed it airily away—'*not* by confusion of substance, but by unity'—they rose, they danced, they triumphed—'by unity, by unity'—they were silent, all but one, and that one fresh perfection proclaimed the full consummation, each syllable rounded, prolonged, exact—'by unity of person' (ch.8, pp.109–10).

[11] *AP* Agathon 5.
[12] Bede, *Eccl Hist* I 30.
[13] *Cels* III 12–13; cf. Gregory Thaumaturgus, *Orig* 151ff.
[14] *Religiöse Bewegungen im Mittelalter* (repr. Darmstadt 1970).
[15] *Schriften zur Theologie*, III, p. 451 (ET K. H. & B. Kruger, *Theological Investigations*, III (London 1967), 'On Conversions to the Church').
[16] *Str* I 57:6, VI 125:3.

Chapter Twelve

[1] Cf. Bernard Bro, *The Little Way* (London 1979), ch. 8. Thérèse, *Hist* V pp.115–17; *DE* 2.9.7 (T p. 353, ET p. 123).
[2] *DE* 11.7.6 (T p. 254, ET pp. 40–1), 20.7.3 (T p. 272, no ET), 6.8.8 (T pp. 308–9, ET p. 89).
[3] *Hist* IV, p. 99.
[4] Ephrem, *HJulSab* 6:22–23. Cf. the use Baudelaire makes of the moral ambiguity of love and art and religion in *Mon Coeur mis à nu*, from which I quote a few passages:

What is art? Prostitution. . . .
Love can derive from a generous feeling: the taste for prostitution.
But it soon gets corrupted by the taste for possession (Pl p. 649, MR p. 623).
The sole and highest pleasure in love lies in the certainty of *doing wrong* (Pl p. 652, MR p. 624).
Of self-cultivation in love, from the point of view of health, hygiene, toilet, spiritual nobility and eloquence.
Self-purification and anti-humanity.

There is in the act of love a great resemblance to torture or to a surgical operation. . . .
God is a scandal (Pl pp. 659–60, MR p. 627).
What is love?
The need to go out of oneself.
Man is an adoring animal.
To adore is to sacrifice oneself and to prostitute oneself.
So all love is prostitution.
The most prostituted being of all is the Being par excellence, God, since he is every individual's supreme friend, the common, inexhaustible reservoir of love (Pl p. 692, MR p. 635).

This last text is followed immediately by a prayer, and is to be taken as a serious religious statement.

[5] Cf. Walter Stein etc, *Nuclear Weapons and Christian Conscience* (London 1961), pp. 111–12.

[6] Cf. *ST* IIa IIae q.23 a.7.

[7] Celsus, in Origen, *Cels* III 5; 8; 14; VIII 2; 49.

[8] E.g. Clement of Alexandria, *Prot* X 89:2, 93:2; Origen, *Cels* I 1, II 1; Gregory of Nyssa, *Virg* III 3 (= J 259:1–2); Theodore of Studios, *Cat. Magn* I 11.

[9] Cf. A. Heschel, *The Prophets* (New York 1969), p. 113.

[10] *HNat* 14:1–6.

[11] *The Imitation of Christ*, I 20:5.

[12] Cf. William of St Thierry, *Gold Ep* 79.

Bibliography

Major critical editions and modern translations of all the works used in this book are listed here, in so far as I have been able to trace them. Occasionally, where there is an abundance of editions. and translations I have not thought it necessary or helpful to mention any of them in particular. Abbreviations used in the Notes to refer to individual works or editions are given here. Except for modern writers and composite works like the Talmud, and two undatable traditional texts (Dhammapada and Bhagavad Gita), I give at least approximate dates for all entries.

ACTS OF DOMINICAN GENERAL CHAPTERS (13th century)
   T: B. M. Reichert (Monumenta Ordinis Praedicatorum Historica 3, Rome 1898).
   No ET.

ACTS OF JOHN (3rd century?)
   T: M. Bonnet, *Acta Apostolorum Apocrypha* II 1 (Leipzig 1898; repr. Hildesheim & New York 1972).
   ET: E. Hennecke, W. Schneemelcher, R. McL. Wilson, *New Testament Apocrypha* II (London 1965).

ACTS OF JUDAS THOMAS (3rd century?)
   T: M. Bonnet, *Acta Apostolorum Apocrypha* II 2 (Leipzig 1903; repr. Hildesheim & New York 1972).
   ET: (a)   E. Hennecke, W. Schneemelcher, R. McL. Wilson, *New Testament Apocrypha* II (London 1965)
         (b)   A. F. J. Klijn, *The Acts of Thomas* (Leiden 1962).

ADVENT LYRICS (9th century?)
 T: G. P. Krapp & E. van Kirk Dobbie, *The Exeter Book (Christ I)* (New York 1936).
 T + ET: J. J. Campbell (Princeton 1959).
 ET: R. K. Gordon, *Anglo-Saxon Poetry* (Everyman, London 1954).

AELRED, St (1109–67)
Sermones Inediti
 T: C. H. Talbot (Rome 1952).
 No ET.

AESCHYLUS (525–456 B.C.)

AMBROSE, St (*c.* 339–97)
Apologia David Altera (= *Apol Dav* 2)
 T: C. Schenkl (Corpus Scriptorum Ecclesiasticorum Latinorum, Louvain 1897).
 No ET.

ANGELUS SILESIUS (1624–77)
Cherubinischer Wandersmann
 Various editions.
 T + FT: H. Plard (Paris 1946).
 No complete ET.

APOPHTHEGMATA PATRUM (4th – 6th centuries) (= *AP*)
 There are two main collections:
 (1)   The Alphabetic Collection.
 T: No critical edition. Text in PG 65, reproduced in P. B. Paschos, *To Gerontikon* (Athens 1961). Supplementary material in J. C. Guy, *Recherches sur la tradition grecque des Apophthegmata Patrum* (Brussels 1962).
 ET: Benedicta Ward (London & Kalamazoo 1975).
 (2)   The Systematic Collection.
 T: Partial edition by M. Nau, *Revue de l'orient Chrétien*, 1908–13.
 ET: Partial translation by Benedicta Ward, *The Wisdom of the Desert Fathers* (Oxford 1975).
 The most complete version of all this material is in the FT by L. Regnault (Solesmes 1966–76), 3 vols.

AP followed by a name refers to (1), followed by Nau refers to (2).

APOSTOLIC CONSTITUTIONS (4th century)
T + LT: F. X. Funk (Paderborn 1905).
ET: ANF vol. 7.

APOSTOLIC FATHERS
Many editions and translations.
T + ET: Kirsopp Lake (LCL 1912–13), 2 vols.

ARISTOTLE (384–322 B.C.)
Nicomachean Ethics (= *Eth Nic*).
Metaphysics (= *Met*).
Various editions and translations.

ASCENSION OF ISAIAH (2nd – 4th centuries)
ET (with details about T):   E. Hennecke, W. Schneemelcher, R. McL. Wilson, *New Testament Apocrypha* II (London 1965)

ATHANASIUS, St (*c.* 296–373)
(1)   *Life of Anthony* (= *VA*).
T: No critical edition of the Greek.
LT: Critical edition of an ancient Latin version, with Italian translation, G. J. M. Bartelink (Mondadori, Florence 1974).
ET: R. T. Meyer (ACW 10, 1950).
(2)   *Contra Gentes* (= *CG*).
T + ET: R. W. Thomson (Oxford 1971).

AUGUSTINE, St (354–430)
There are many editions and translations, of which only a few are mentioned below. For T, look in any complete edition of Augustine.
(1)   *The Lord's Sermon on the Mount* (= *SDM*).
ET: (a)   J. J. Jepson (ACW 5, 1948).
      (b)   D. J. Kavanagh (FC 1951).
(2)   *Confessions* (= *Conf*).
(3)   *On the Trinity* (= *Trin*).
ET: S. McKenna (FC 1963).
(4)   *On the City of God* (= *CD*).
(5)   *Discourses on the Psalms* (= *Enarr in Ps*).
(6)   *Sermons* (= *Serm*).

BABYLONIAN TALMUD (= *BT*)
ET: Soncino edition (London 1935, in 35 vols, repr. 1961 in 18 vols).

I refer to and quote from this edition. Abbreviations of individual tractates are in accordance with those used in this edition. A useful selection of Rabbinic material can be found also in A. Cohen, *Everyman's Talmud* (= *EvT*).

BAKER, Augustine (1575–1641)
Commentary on the Cloud of Unknowing.

Ed. and adapted by J. McCann, *The Cloud of Unknowing* (London 1924).

BARNABAS, Letter of (early 2nd century)
In most editions and translations of the Apostolic Fathers.

T + FT: P. Prigent & R. A. Kraft (SC 172, 1971).

BASIL, St (*c.* 330–79)
(1) *Long Rules* (= *RF*).

T: No critical edition.

ET: M. M. Wagner (FC 1950).

(2) *Letters* (= *Ep*).

T + FT: Y. Courtonne (Budé 1957–66), 3 vols.

T + ET: R. J. Deferrari (LCL 1926–34), 4 vols.

ET: A. C. Way (FC 1951–5), 2 vols.

(3) *Homilies on the Six Days of Creation* (= *Hex*).

T + FT: S. Giet (SC 26, 1968).

ET: NPNF II vol. viii.

(4) *On the Holy Spirit* (= *Spir*).

T + FT: B. Pruche (SC17, 1968).

ET: NPNF II vol. viii.

BAUDELAIRE, Charles (1821–67)
Of the various editions of his works, I refer to two:

(1) *Oeuvres complètes*, ed. C. Pichois (Bibliothèque de la Pléiade, Paris 1975) (= Pl).

(2) *Oeuvres complètes*, ed. M. A. Ruff (Paris 1968) (= MR).

BEDE, St (*c.* 673–735)
Ecclesiastical History (= *Eccl Hist*).

T + ET: B. Colgrave and R. A. B. Mynors (Oxford 1969).

BERNARD, St (1090–1153)

There is a critical edition in progress, ed. J. Leclercq and others (Rome 1957ff). There are various translations of most of his works, including a new one in progress from CF.

(1) *Letters* (= *Ep*).

ET: B. S. James (London 1953).

(2) *On the Canticle* (= *Cant*).

T: Vols. i–ii (1957–8)

(3) *Sermons on the Assumption* (= *Serm Ass*).

T: Vol. v (1968).

BHAGAVAD GITA

T + ET: R. C. Zaehner (Oxford 1969).

BLAKE, William (1757–1827)

BOCCACCIO, Giovanni (1313–75)

Il Filostrato.

T: Vincenzo Pernicone (Bari 1937)

No ET.

BOETHIUS (*c*.480–*c*.524)

Consolation of Philosophy.

Various editions and translations.

BOSSUET, J.-B. (1627–1704)

Méditations sur l'Évangile (= *Méd Év*).

T: M. Dreano (Paris 1966).

No ET.

CASSIAN (*c*. 360–435)

Institutes (= *Inst*).

T + FT: J. C. Guy (SC 109, 1965).

ET: NPNF II vol. xi.

CATHERINE OF SIENA, St (1347–80)

Dialogue (= *Dial*).

T: G. Cavallini (Rome 1968).

ET: A. Thorold (London 1896).

CAUSSADE, J. P. de (1675–1751)

(1) *L'Abandon à la providence divine* (= *Ab*).

T: M. Olphe-Galliard (Paris 1966)

159

ET: All English translations known to me are based on Ramière's rearrangement of the text, and therefore have different chapter numbers from those in T. The chapter numbers given in the Notes refer to Ramière's arrangement, the page numbers to T.

(2) *Lettres spirituelles* (= *Lettres*).

T: M. Olphe-Galliard (Paris 1962–4), 2 vols.

ET: There are 3 vols. of Letters, translated from Ramière and therefore not corresponding to T. They are all by A. Thorold.

(a) *The Spiritual Letters of Fr J. P. de Caussade* (London 1934) (= ET 1934).

(b) *Ordeals of Souls* (London 1936) (= ET 1936).

(c) *Comfort in Ordeals* (London 1937).

CAVAFY, Constantine (1863–1933)

Notes on Ruskin

I have not been able to see *Anekdota Peza*, ed. M. Peridis (Athens 1963), which I presume contains the original of this text. There is an ET of parts of it in R. Liddell, *Cavafy* (London 1974), pp. 116–17.

CHAUCER, Geoffrey (*c.* 1343–1400)

Troilus and Criseyde.

T: In all editions of Chaucer.

ET: Nevill Coghill (Penguin Classics 1971).

CHESTERTON, G. K. (1874–1936)

The Innocence of Father Brown.

I quote from the Penguin edition (1950).

CHRISTIE, Agatha

Absent in the Spring (under the name of Mary Westmacott).

I quote from the Fontana edition (1974).

CHRYSIPPUS (*c.* 280–*c.*207 B.C.)

T: Fragments in J. von Arnim, *Stoicorum Veterum Fragmenta* II & III (Leipzig 1903, repr. Stuttgart 1968) (= *SVF*).

CHRYSOSTOM, St John (*c.* 347–407)

Baptismal Catecheses (= *Cat*).

T + FT: A. Wenger (SC 50, 1957)

ET: P. W. Harkins (ACW 31, 1963).

CLEMENT

(So-called) 2 Clement (2nd century)
In most editions and translations of the Apostolic Fathers.

CLEMENT OF ALEXANDRIA (c.150–c.215)

T: O. Stählin & L. Früchtel (GCS 1960–72), 3 vols.
(1) *Who is the Rich Man who is Saved?* (= *QDS*).
T: Vol. iii.
T + ET: G. W. Butterworth (LCL 1919)
(2) *Stromateis* (= *Str*).
T: Vols. ii & iii.
ET: ANF vol. ii.
ET of *Str* VII: J. E. L. Oulton & H. Chadwick, *Alexandrian Christianity* (London 1954).
(3) *Protrepticus* (= *Prot*).
T: Vol. i.
T + ET: G. W. Butterworth (LCL 1919).

CLOUD OF UNKNOWING (14th century)

And other works by the same anonymous author.
T: Phyllis Hodgson (Early English Text Society OS 218, 231, 1944, 1955).
ET: A full modern version is being prepared by J. Walsh for CWS. Meantime several of the works are contained in the new Penguin Classics translation by C. Wolters (1978).

CYRIL OF ALEXANDRIA, St (died 444)

That Christ is One (= *Quod Chr Unus*).
T + FT: G. M. de Durand (SC 97, 1964).
ET: *On the Incarnation against Nestorius* (LF 1881).

CYRIL OF JERUSALEM, St (c. 315–86)

Catecheses (= *Cat*).
T: W. K. Reischl & J. Rupp (Munich 1848–60).
ET: L. P. McCaulay & A. A. Stephenson (FC 1969, 1970).

DHAMMAPADA

T + ET: Narada Maha Thera (Calcutta 1952).
I quote from this edition.

DICKINSON, Emily (1830–86)

Critical edition of the poems by T. H. Johnson (Harvard 1963), 3 vols.

DIDACHE (1st century)
In most editions of the Apostolic Fathers.
T + FT: W. Rordorf & A. Tuilier (SC 248, 1978).

DIDASCALIA (3rd century)
ET: H. Connolly (Oxford, 1929).
I refer to this edition.

DIOGNETUS, Letter to (2nd century)
In most editions of the Apostolic Fathers.
T + FT: H. I. Marrou (SC 33, 1965).

DIONYSIUS (Pseudo-) (5th–6th century)
On the Divine Names (= Div Nom)
T: No critical edition.
ET: C. E. Rolt (London 1920).

DOMINIC, St (1170–1221)
(Anon.), *The Nine Ways of Prayer of St Dominic (= Nine Ways)*.
T: I. Taurisano (Analecta Ordinis Praedicatorum (15) 1922).
ET: Simon Tugwell (Dublin 1978).

DURANDUS OF SAINT-POURÇAIN (*c.* 1275–1334)
Commentary on the Sentences (= in Sent.).
T: Venice 1571 (Gregg reprint 1964).
No ET.

ECKHART, Meister (*c.* 1260–1327)
T: There is a critical edition of the German works in progress, ed. J. Quint (Stuttgart 1958ff) (= QMa).
GT: Modern German version of the works considered authentic, by J. Quint (Munich 1963) (= QMi).
ET: (a)   J. M. Clark, *Meister Eckhart, An Introduction* (Nelson, London 1957) (= ClNel).
       (b)   J. M. Clark & J. V. Skinner, *Meister Eckhart, Selected Treatises and Sermons* (Faber, London 1958) (= ClFab).
       (c)   Reprint of (b) by Fontana 1963 (= ClFon).
       (d)   M. O'C. Walshe, *Meister Eckhart*, vol. i (London 1979) (= W).

Since there is no uniform way of referring to texts, I cite as many of the above as are available, with the abbreviations indicated. The edition and translations listed here supersede all others previously published. (d) is the first volume of a projected complete translation.

Only where no modern ET is available do I refer to F. Pfeiffer & C. de B. Evans, *Meister Eckhart* (London 1924, 1931), an edition that must be used with caution (= PE).

EPHREM, St (*c*.306–73)
(1) *Commentary on the Diatessaron.*
T + LT: L. Leloir (Dublin 1963)
FT: L. Leloir (SC 121, 1966).
No ET.
(2) *Commentary on Genesis.*
T + LT: R. M. Tonneau (CSCO 152–3, 1955).
No ET.
(3) *Hymns on Faith* (= *HFid*).
T + GT: E. Beck (CSCO 154–5, 1955).
ET: J. B. Morris, *Selected Works* (Oxford 1847).
(4) *Hymns on Julian Saba* (= *HJulSab*).
T + GT: E. Beck (CSCO 322–3, 1972).
No ET.
(5) *Hymns on the Nativity* (= *HNat*).
T + GT: E. Beck (CSCO 186–7, 1959).
No ET.

EPICTETUS (*c*.55–*c*.135)
T + ET: W. A. Oldfather (LCL 1926–8), 2 vols.

ESDRAS
4 Esdras (*c*. A.D. 100)
T: (a)   R. L. Bensly (Texts & Studies, Cambridge 1895).
       (b)   Bruno Violet (GCS, 1910).
ET: R. M. Charles, *Apocrypha and Pseudepigrapha of the Old Testament* II (Oxford 1913).

EURIPIDES (*c*.485–*c*.406 B.C.)

EUSEBIUS (*c*.260–*c*.340)
Preparation for the Gospel (= *PE*).
T + ET: E. H. Gifford (Oxford 1903)

EVAGRIUS PONTICUS (346–99)

(1) *Praktikos* (= *Prakt*).

T + FT: A. & C. Guillaumont (SC 170–1, 1971).

ET: J. E. Bamberger (Cistercian Publications 1970).

(2) *Kephalaia Gnostica* (= *KG*).

T + FT: A. Guillaumont (PO XXVIII 1; 1958).

No ET.

(3) *On Prayer* (= *Or*).

T: No critical edition. The text is found in PG 79 and *Philokalia* I.

ET: (a) J. E. Bamberger (Cistercian Publications 1970).

  (b) G. E. H. Palmer, P. Sherrard & K. Ware, *The Philo-kalia*, I (London 1979), pp. 55–71.

(4) *Letter* (= *Ep 8*).

Letter 8 in the collection of Basil's letters is almost certainly to be ascribed to Evagrius. For editions, see under BASIL.

FABER, F. W. (1814–63)

The Creator and the Creature (London 1856).

GOSPEL OF THOMAS (2nd century)

T + ET: A. Guillaumont, H. C. Puech, etc. (Leiden 1959).

I quote from this translation.

GOSPEL OF TRUTH (2nd century)

T: M. Malinine, H. C. Puech, G. Quispel, *Evangelium Veritatis* (Zürich 1956).

ET: (a) J. M. Robinson, *The Nag Hammadi Library in English* (Leiden & San Francisco 1977)

  (b) W. Förster & R. McL. Wilson, *Gnosis* II (Oxford 1974).

GREENE, Graham

The Power and the Glory.

I quote from the Penguin edition (1971).

GREGORY THE GREAT, St (*c.* 540–604)

(1) *Morals on Job* (= *Mor*(.

T: A critical edition is in progress by R. Gillet & A. de Gaudemaris in SC.

ET: LF (1844ff).

(2) *Homilies on the Gospels* (= *Hom in Ev.*).

GREGORY OF NYSSA, St (*c*.330–*c*.395)

A critical edition, started by W. Jaeger, is in progress (Leiden 1952ff) (= J).

(1)   *On Virginity* (= *Virg*).
T: J vol. viii.
T + FT: M. Aubineau (SC 119, 1966).
ET: V. W. Callahan, *Ascetical Works* (FC, 1967).
(2)   *Life of Moses* (= *VM*).
T: J vol. vii, 1.
T + FT: J. Daniélou (SC 1, 1955).
ET: A. J. Malherbe & E. Fergusson (CWS 1978).
(3)   *On the Canticle* (= *Cant*).
T: J vol. vi.
No ET.
(4)   *On Ecclesiastes* (= *Eccl*).
T: J vol. v.
No ET.

GREGORY THAUMATURGUS, St (*c*.213–*c*.270)

Farewell Discourse to Origen (= *Orig*).
T + FT: H. Crouzel (SC 148, 1969).
ET: W. Metcalfe (London 1920).

For a strong argument against the traditional ascription of this speech to Gregory, see P. Nautin, *Origène* I (Paris 1977), pp. 80ff.

GUERRIC (became abbot of Igny in 1138)

T + FT: J. Morson, H. Costello, P. Deseille (SC 166, 202, 1970–3), 2 vols.
ET: Monks of Mount St Bernard's Abbey (CF 8, 32, 1971), 2 vols.

GUIGO I (1083–1136)

Meditations.
T + FT: A. Wilmart, *Le Recueil des pensées de B. Guigue* (Paris 1936).
ET: J. J. Jolin (Milwaukee 1951).

GUIGO II (died 1188)

The Ladder of Monks (= *Scala*).
T + FT: E. Colledge & J. Walsh (SC 163, 1970).
ET: E. Colledge & J. Walsh (Oxford 1978).

GUTHLAC (9th century?)

T: G. P. Krapp & E. van Kirk Dobbie, *The Exeter Book* (New York 1936).

ET: R. K. Gordon, *Anglo-Saxon Poetry* (Everyman, London 1954).

HEINE, Heinrich (1797–1856)

HERACLITUS (*flor. c.* 500 B.C.)

T + GT of fragments: H. Diels & W. Kranz, *Die Fragmente der Vorsokratiker* (Berlin 1952) (= DK).

T + ET: M. Marcovich (Merida 1967) (= M).

ET: K. Freeman, *Ancilla to the Presocratic Philosophers* (Oxford 1948).

HERMAS (2nd century)

In most editions of the Apostolic Fathers.

T + FT: R. Joly (SC 53, 1968).

I gave references both to Joly's system of paragraphs and to the older divisions, using standard abbreviations.

HERMES TRISMEGISTUS (1st – 3rd centuries)

T + ET: W. Scott (Oxford 1924).

T + FT: A. D. Nock & A. J. Festugière (Budé 1946–54), 4 vols.

HERRICK Robert (1591–1674)

HUGH OF FOUILLOY (*c.* 1110–72)

Cloister of the Soul.

No critical edition or ET.

HUGH OF ST VICTOR (died 1142)

Miscellanies.

No critical edition or ET.

IGNATIUS OF ANTIOCH, St (early 2nd century)

In most editions of the Apostolic Fathers.

T + FT: P. Th. Camelot (SC 10, 1969).

IONESCO, Eugene

Un Homme en question (Paris 1979).

IRENAEUS, St (*c.*130–*c.*200)

(1) *Against the Heresies* (= *a.H.*).

T + FT: A new critical edition, which will supersede all previous editions, is in progress, ed. A. Rousseau and others. So far Books 3–5 have been published (SC 211, 100, 153, 1965–74).

T: W. W. Harvey (Cambridge 1857), 2 vols.

ET: ANF vol. i.

(2) *Demonstration of the Apostolic Preaching* (= *Dem*).

ET (from Armenian): J. P. Smith (ACW 16, 1952).

JOSEPHUS (*c*.37–*c*.100)
Jewish War (= *Bell Jud*).

T + ET: H. St J. Thackeray & R. Marcus (LCL 1926ff).

JULIAN OF NORWICH (*c*. 1343–after 1413)

T: E. Colledge & J. Walsh, *A Book of Showings to the Anchoress Julian of Norwich* (Toronto 1978).

ET: The main complete modern version is by E. Colledge & J. Walsh (CWS 1978).

Both of these contain both the Short Text and the Long Text. All my references are to the Long Text.

LEWIS, C. S. (1898–1963)

(1) *The Screwtape Letters* (London 1942)

(2) *The Pilgrim's Regress* (London 1933). I refer to the Fount edition (1977).

(3) *Williams and the Arthuriad* (originally *Arthurian Torso*, etc., Oxford 1948) repr. with C. Williams, *Taliessin through Logres* (Grand Rapids 1974). I refer to the 1974 edition.

(4) *Voyage to Venus* (originally *Perelandra*, London 1943). I quote from the Pan edition (1953).

(6) *Letters to Arthur Greeves* (ed. W. Hooper, *They Stand Together*, London 1979).

(6) *The Allegory of Love* (Oxford 1936)

(7) *The Great Divorce* (London 1946). I refer to the Fontana edition (1972).

LIBER GRADUUM (5th century?)

T + LT: M. Kmosko (*PS* 3, 1926).

No ET.

LIVES OF THE BRETHREN (1259–60)

T: B. M. Reichert (Louvain 1896).

ET: Placid Conway (Newcastle 1896).

MACARIUS (Pseudo-) (4th century).
(1)   *Fifty Spiritual Homilies.*
T: H. Dörries, E. Klostermann, M. Kroeger (Berlin 1964).
ET: A. J. Mason (London 1921).
(2)   T: *Neue Homilien des Makarius/Symeon, aus Typus III*, ed. E. Klostermann & H. Berthold (Berlin 1961) (= *III*).
(3)   T: *Makarius/Symeon, Reden und Briefe*, ed. H. Berthold (GCS 1973).
No ET of (2) and (3).

MACDONALD, George (1824–1905)
Lilith.
I quote from the Ballantine edition (London & New York 1969).

MARVELL, Andrew (1621–78)

MAY, Rollo
(1)   *Love and Will* (= *LW*).
(2)   *Power and Innocence* (= *PI*).
I quote from the Fontana edition, respectively 1972 and 1976.

METHODIUS, St (died *c.* 311)
Symposium (= *Symp*).
T + FT: H. Musorillo & V. H. Debidour (SC 95, 1963).
ET: H. Musorillo (ACW 27, 1958).

MIDRASH ON PSALMS
ET: W. G. Braude (Yale 1959), 2 vols.
I refer to this edition.

MIDRASH RABBAH (= MR).
ET: Soncino edition (London 1939), 10 vols.
I refer to this edition.

MISHNAH
ET: H. Danby (Oxford 1933)
I refer to this edition.

MISSALE GALLICANUM VETUS
T: L. C. Mohlberg (Rome 1958).
No ET.

NATHAN (3rd century?)
The Fathers according to Rabbi Nathan.
ET: J. Goldin (Yale 1955). I quote from the Schocken edition (New York 1974).

NUMENIUS (2nd century A.D.)
T + FT of the fragments: E. des Places (Budé 1973).
No ET.

ORIGEN (*c.*185–*c.*254)
The only critical edition of all the works is in GCS, by various editors.
There is no complete ET.
(1) *On Prayer* (= *Or*).
T: GCS vol. ii (1899).
ET: (a) E. G. Jay (London 1954)
(b) J. J. O'Meara (ACW 19, 1954).
(c) J. E. L. Oulton & H. Chadwick, *Alexandrian Christianity* (London 1954).
(d) R. A. Greer (CWS 1979).
(2) *Against Celsus* (= *Cels*).
T: GCS vols. i–ii (1899).
T + FT: M. Borret (SC 132, 136, 147, 150, 227, 1967–76).
ET: H. Chadwick (Cambridge 1953).
(3) *Commentary on Matthew* (= *Comm in Matt*).
T: GCS vol. x (1935).
No ET.
(4) *Commentary on Matthew (Latin fragments)* (= *Ser in Matt*).
T: GCS vol. xi (1933).
No ET.
(5) *On First Principles* (= *Princ*).
T: GCS vol. v (1913).
ET: G. W. Butterworth (London 1936; repr. New York 1966).
(6) *Homilies on Joshuah* (= *Josh*).
T: GCS vol. vii (1921).
T + FT: A. Jaubert (SC 71, 1960).
No ET.
(7) *Philokalia* (= *Phil*).
T: J. A. Robinson (Cambridge 1893).
T + FT of *Phil* 21–7: E. Junod (SC 226, 1976).

No ET.
(8)   *Exhortation to Martyrdom* (= *Mart*).
T: GCS vol. i (1899).
ET: (a)   J. J. O'Meara (ACW 19, 1954).
       (b)   Oulton & Chadwick, op. cit.
       (c)   R. A. Greer (CWS 1979).
(9)   *Commentary on the Canticle* (= *Cant*).
T: GCS vol. viii (1925).
ET: R. P. Lawson (ACW 26, 1957).
ET of the Prologue: R. A. Greer (CWS 1979)
(10)   *Homilies on Numbers* (= *Num*).
T: GCS vol. vii (1921).
FT: A. Méhat (SC 29, 1951).
ET of Homily 27:   R. A. Greer (CWS 1979).

PELAGIUS (*flor. c.* 400)
Letter to Demetrias (= *Dem*).
No critical edition or ET.

PETER CALO (died 1348)
Life of St Thomas Aquinas.
T: D. Prümmer, *Fontes Vitae S. Thomae* (Toulouse 1911).
No ET.

PHILO (*c.*20 B.C. – *c.* A.D. 50)
T + ET: F. H. Colson & G. H. Whittaker (LCL 1929 ff), 10 vols.
I use standard abbreviations for particular works.

PLATO (*c.* 429–347 B.C.)

POSIDONIUS (*c.*135–*c.*50 B.C.)
T of fragments: L. Edelstein & I. G. Kidd (Cambridge 1972).
No ET.

PROCLUS (*c.*410–85).
Platonic Theology (= *Plat Theol*)
T + FT: H. D. Saffrey & L. G. Westerink (Budé 1968ff, in progress).
No ET.

RAYMUND OF CAPUA, Bl (*c.*1330–99)

Life of Catherine of Siena.
T: *Acta Sanctorum* XII (Paris & Rome 1866)
ET: Conleth Kearns (Wilmington, USA, 1980).

RIMBAUD, Arthur (1854–91)
T + ET: *Complete Works and Selected Letters,* tr. Wallace Fowlie (Chicago 1966).

ROMANOS THE MELODIST, St (*flor. c.*540)
T: *Cantica Genuina,* ed. P. Maas & C. A. Trypanis (Oxford 1963) (= MT).
T + FT: J. G. de Matons (SC 99, 110, 114, 128, 1964–67) (= SC).
ET: M. Carpenter (Columbia 1970ff).

SENECA (*c.*4 B.C. – A.D. 65)
Letters to Lucilius (= *Ep*).

SERAPION (4th century)
Prayer Book.
T + LT: F. X. Funk, *Didascalia et Constitutiones Apostolorum* (Paderborn 1905) II.
ET: J. Wordsworth, *Bishop Sarapion's Prayer Book* (London 1899).

SEXTUS EMPIRICUS (*flor. c.*200?)
T + ET: R. G. Bury (LCL 1933ff), 4 vols.
I use standard abbreviations to refer to particular works.

SIBYLLINE ORACLES (2nd century)
T: J. Geffcken (GCS 1902).
ET of book viii: E. Hennecke, W. Schneemelcher, R. McL. Wilson, *New Testament Apocrypha* II (London 1965).

SUSO, Bl Henry (*c.* 1295–1366)
Little Book of Truth.
T: K. Bihlmeyer (Stuttgart 1907).
ET: J. M. Clark, *Little Book of Eternal Wisdom and Little Book of Truth* (London 1953).

TELES (*flor. c.*235 B.C.)
T: O. Hense (Tübingen 1909)
T + ET: E. N. O'Neil (Montana 1977).

TERTULLIAN (*c*.160–*c*.225)

(1) *On the Resurrection* (= *Res*).
T + ET: E. Evans (London 1960).
(2) *On Baptism* (= *Bapt*).
T + ET: E. Evans (London 1964).

THEODORE OF STUDIOS, St (759–826)

I refer to a quotation from the *Great Catechesis*, of which an edition is promised, in J. Leroy, *Saint Théodore Studite*, in *Théologie de la vie monastique* (Ligugé 1961), pp. 428 n. 38.

THEOPHILUS OF ANTIOCH, St (2nd century).

To Autolycus (= *Aut*).
T + ET: R. M. Grant (Oxford 1970).

THÉRÈSE OF LISIEUX, St (1873–97)

The critical edition is published by Desclée de Brouwer and Éditions du Cerf, and it is to this that I refer.
(1) *Derniers Entretiens* (= *DE*).
T: 1971
ET: *Novissima Verba*, tr. Carmelite Nuns of New York (Dublin 1953).
(2) *Histoire d'une âme, manuscrits autobiographiques* (= *Hist*).
T: 1979.
ET: There are numerous translations, usually entitled, *The Story of a Soul*.
(3) *Correspondance générale* (= *CG*).
T: 1972–3, 2 vols.
ET: F. J. Sheed, *Collected Letters* (London 1949).

THOMAS À KEMPIS (*c*.1380–1471)

The Imitation of Christ.

THOMAS AQUINAS, St (*c*.1225–74)

There are several editions of the works referred to here. Bibliographical information on all editions and translations into English can be found in J. A. Weisheipl, *Friar Thomas d'Aquino* (Oxford 1975), pp. 357ff.
(1) *Summa Theologiae* (= *ST*).
T + ET: Blackfriars edition (London & New York 1964ff), 60 vols.

(2)   *De Potentia* (= *de Pot*).
ET: English Dominican Fathers, *On the Power of God* (London 1932–4), 3 vols.
(3)   *Lectures on Matthew* (= *in Matt*).
T: I refer to the Marietti edition by R. Cai (Turin 1951).
ET: None.
(4)   *Summa contra Gentiles* (= *CG*).
ET: *On the Truth of the Catholic Faith*, tr. A. C. Pegis, etc. (New York 1955–7), 5 vols.
(5)   *Quodlibetal Questions* (= *Quodl*).
No ET.
(6)   *Commentary on Aristotle's de Anima* (= *Ar, Anim*).
ET: K. Foster & S. Humphries (Yale 1951).
(7)   *De Malo*
No ET.

THOMAS CANTIPRATANUS (*c*.1201–*c*.1270)
De Apibus.
'   I refer to the Douai edition (1605).
No ET.

TRAHERNE, Thomas (*c*.1636–74)
Centuries.
   T: H. M. Margoliouth (Oxford 1958).

VINCENT FERRER, St (*c*.1350–1419)
On the Spiritual Life (= *Vit Spir*).
   T: P. Fages, *Oeuvres de S. Vincent Ferrier* (Paris 1909).
   ET: Dominican nuns of Corpus Christi Monastery, California (London 1957).

WILLIAM OF ST THIERRY (*c*.1085–1148)
(1)   *On the Canticle* (= *Cant*).
T + FT: J. M. Déchanet & M. Dumontier (SC 82, 1962).
ET: C. Hart (CF 6, 1970).
(2)   *Golden Epistle* (= *Gold Ep*).
T + FT: J. M. Déchanet (SC 223, 1975).
ET: T. Berkeley (CF 12, 1971).

WILLIAM OF TOCCO (died after 1323)
Life of St Thomas Aquinas.

T: D. Prümmer, *Fontes Vitae S. Thomae* (Toulouse 1924).
No ET.

WILLIAMS, Charles (1886–1945)

(1)   *He Came down from Heaven* (London 1938; repr. with *The Forgiveness of Sins*, London 1950).

(2)   *Taliessin through Logres* (Oxford 1938; repr. with other material, Grand Rapids 1974).

(3)   *The Figure of Beatrice* (London 1943).

(4)   *The Greater Trumps* (London 1932; repr. 1954). I quote from the 1954 edition.

Index of Scriptural Passages

OLD TESTAMENT

Index of Names